You can contact Sukant Khurana through any of these links:
https://www.facebook.com/SukantKhuranaauthorsite
https://www.facebook.com/Sukant-1625360857788363/
https://twitter.com/sukant_khurana
http://www.brainnart.com
makingviaunmaking@gmail.com

Printed by Create Space 2017

ISBN-13: 978-1542377072

ISBN-10: 1542377072

About this photo-journal

A small attempt at poetry through photographs, using pictures of Long Island, NY, USA. I have intentionally left out beautiful people, identifiable buildings and focussed my lens on heavens and earth.

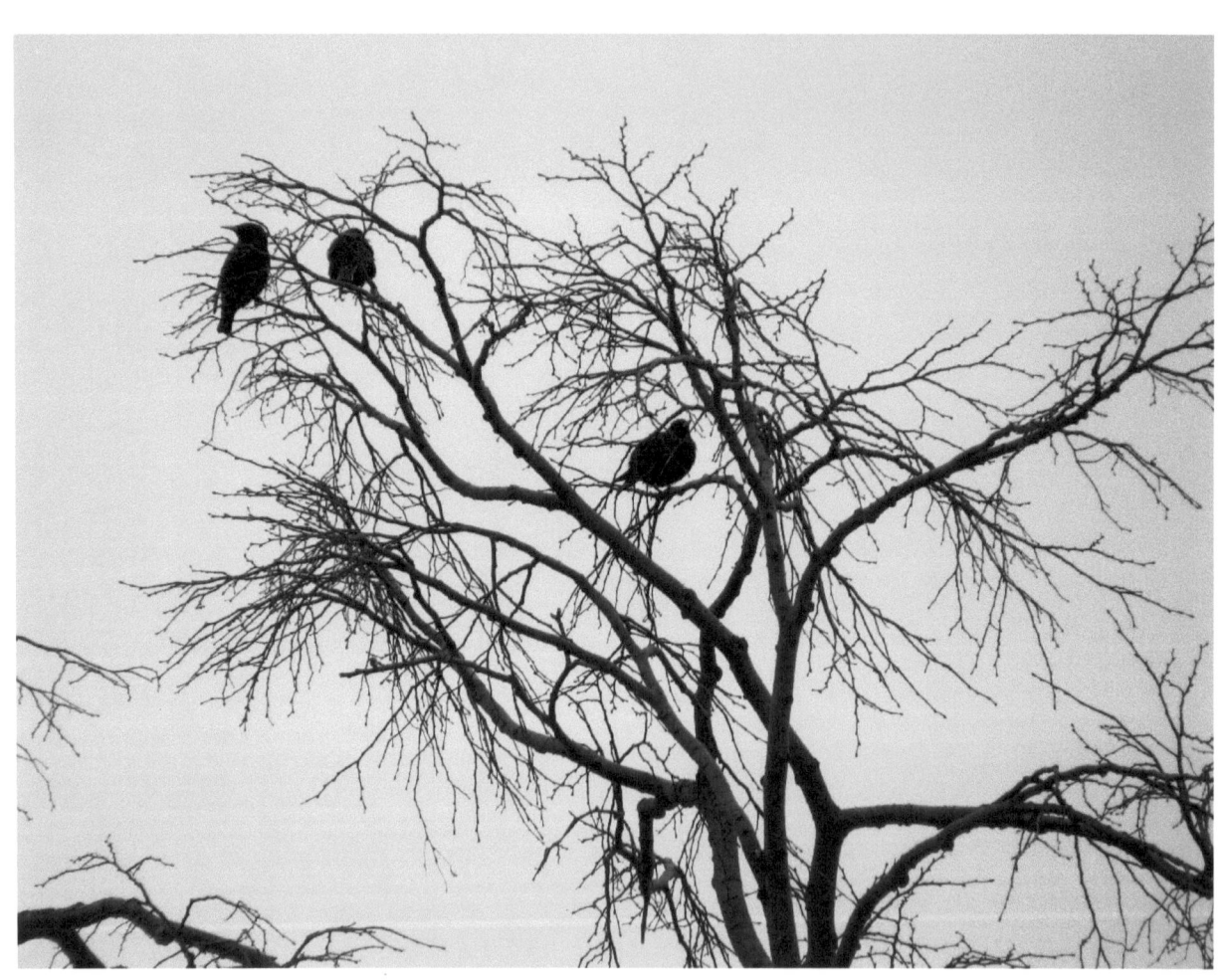

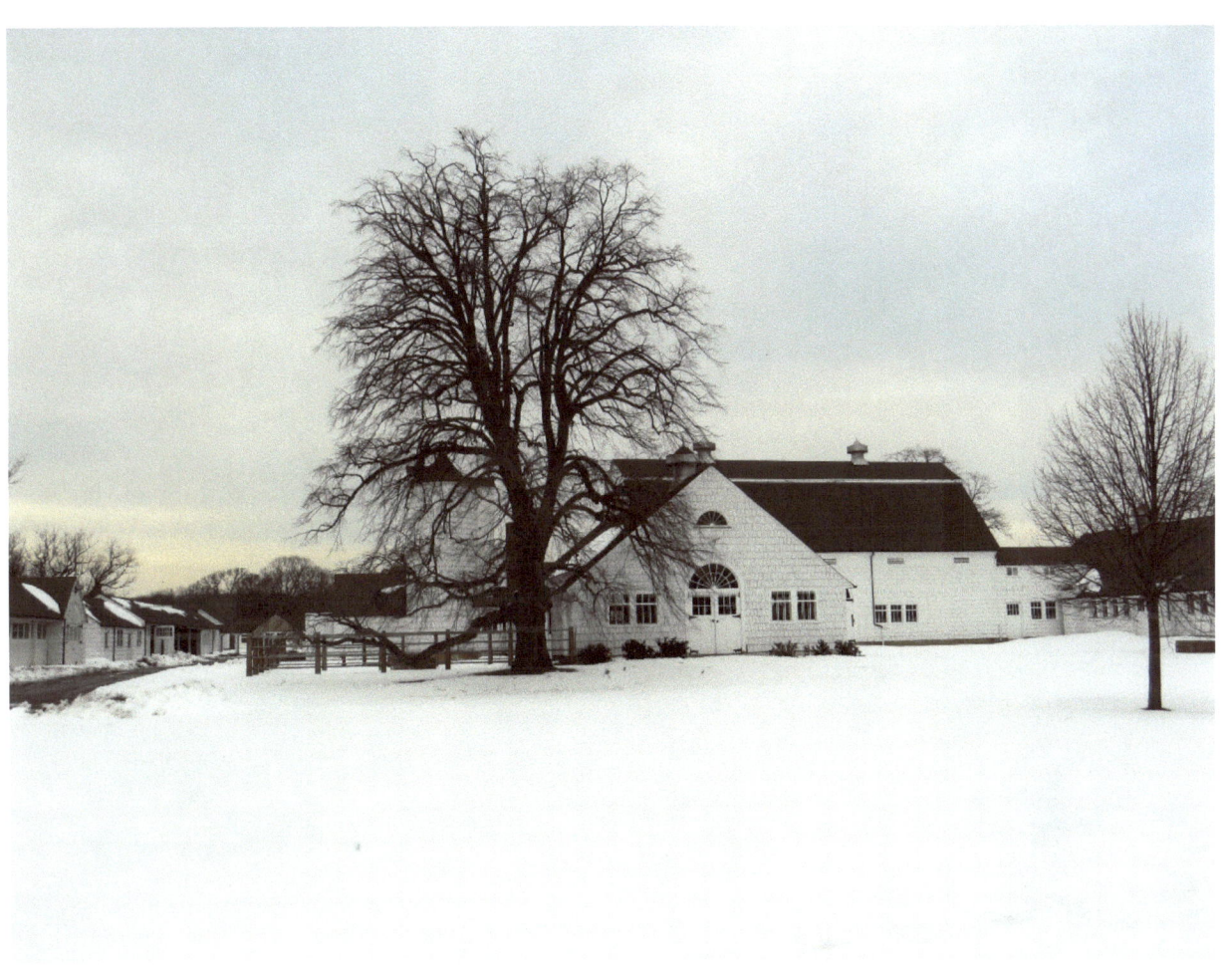

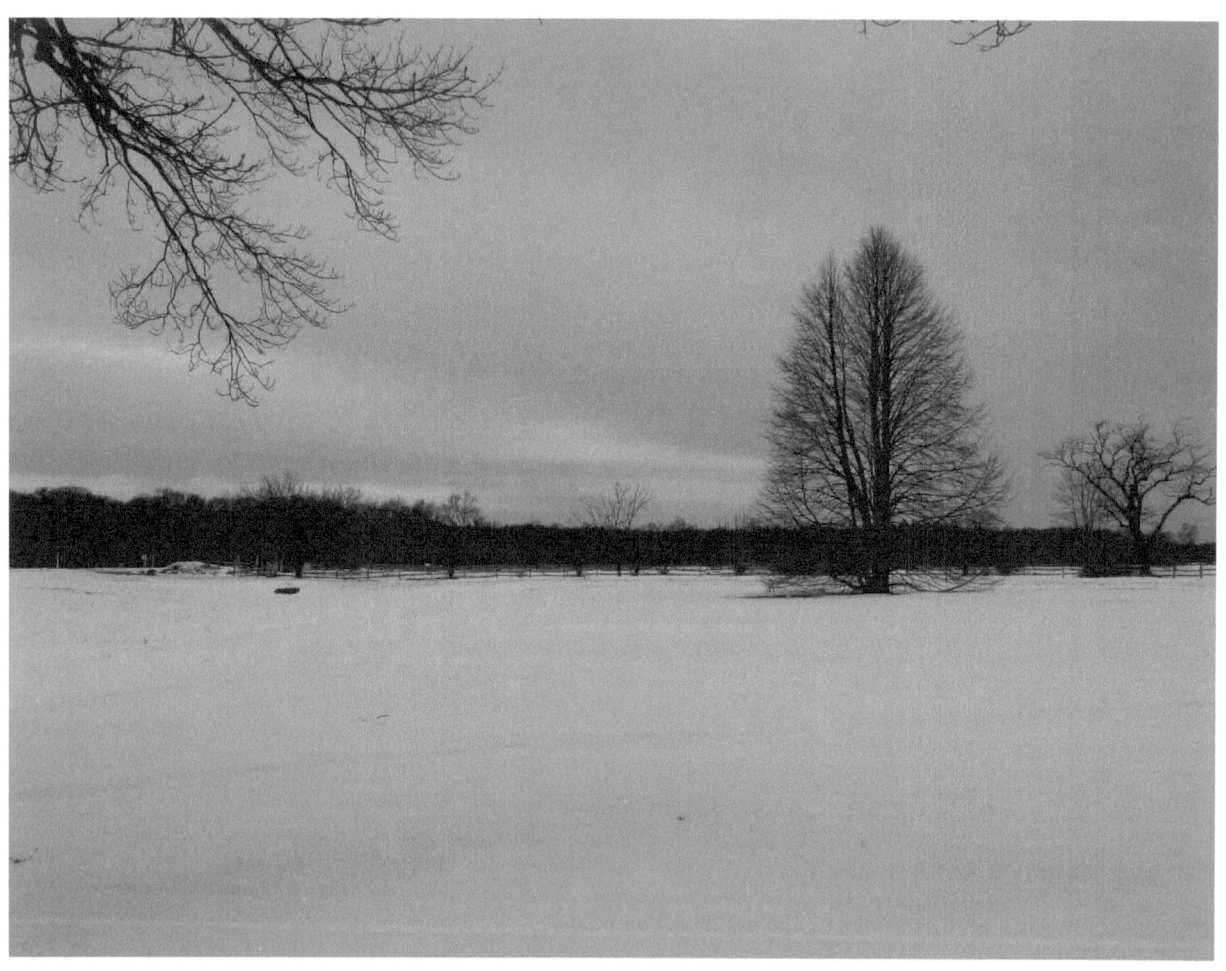

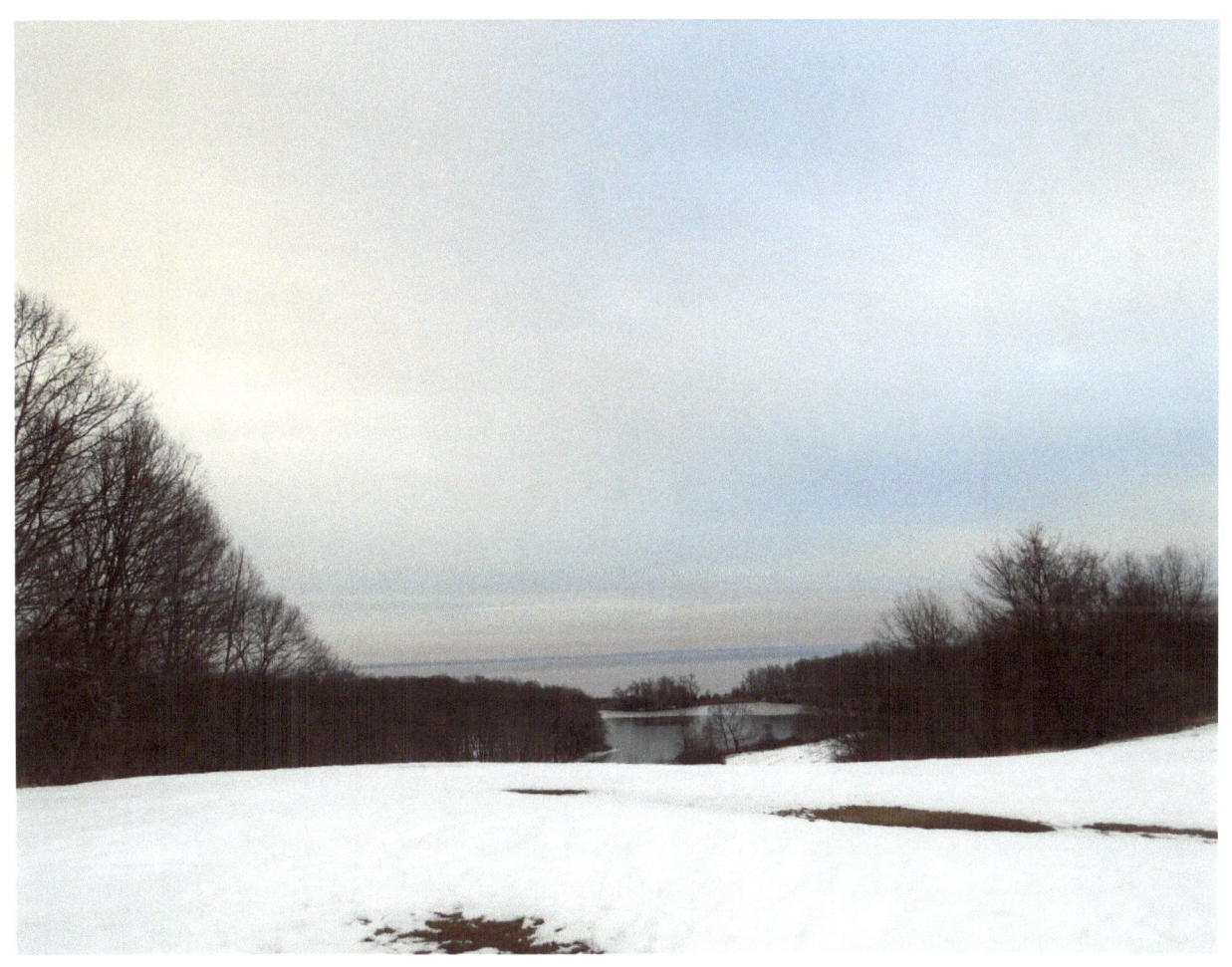

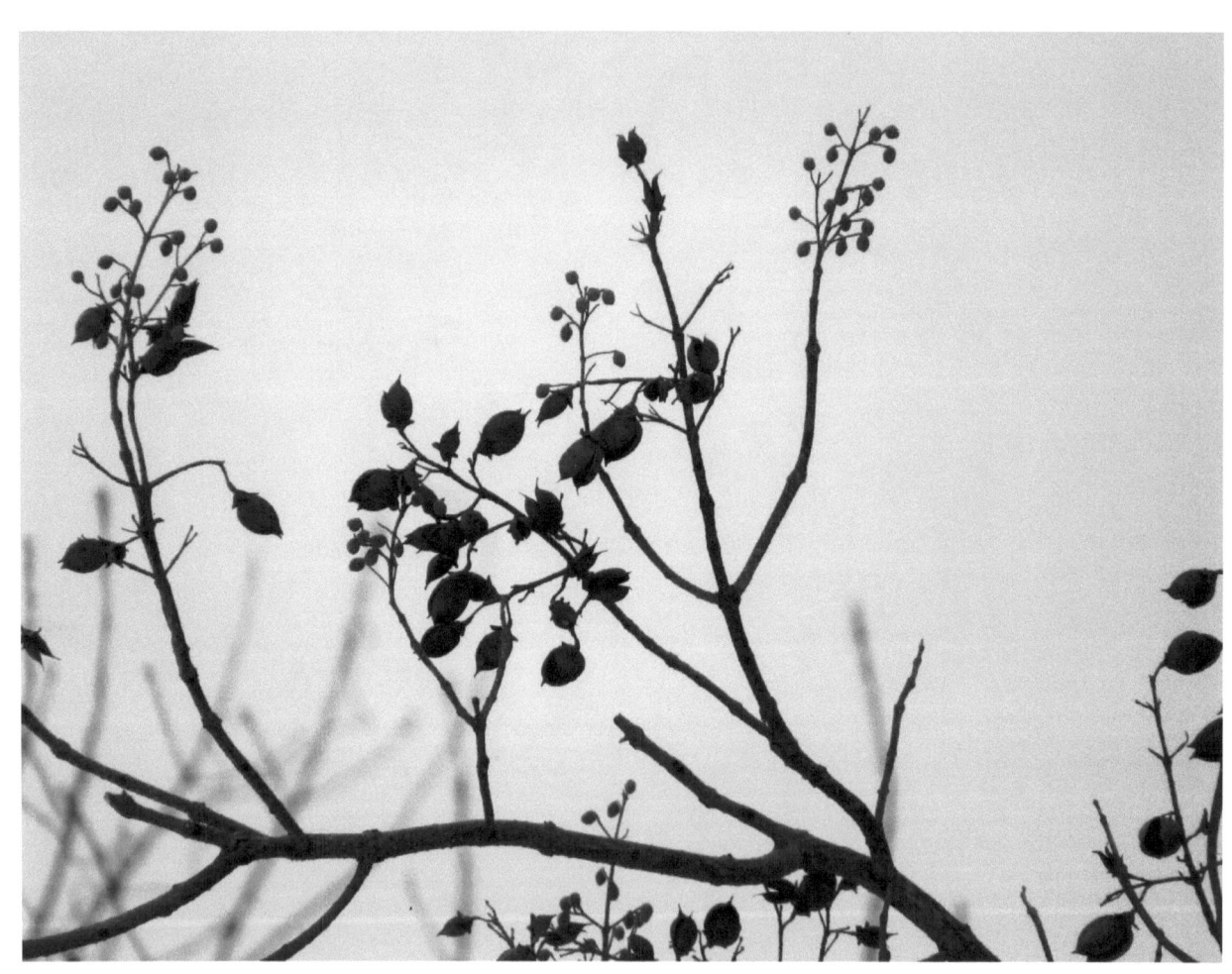

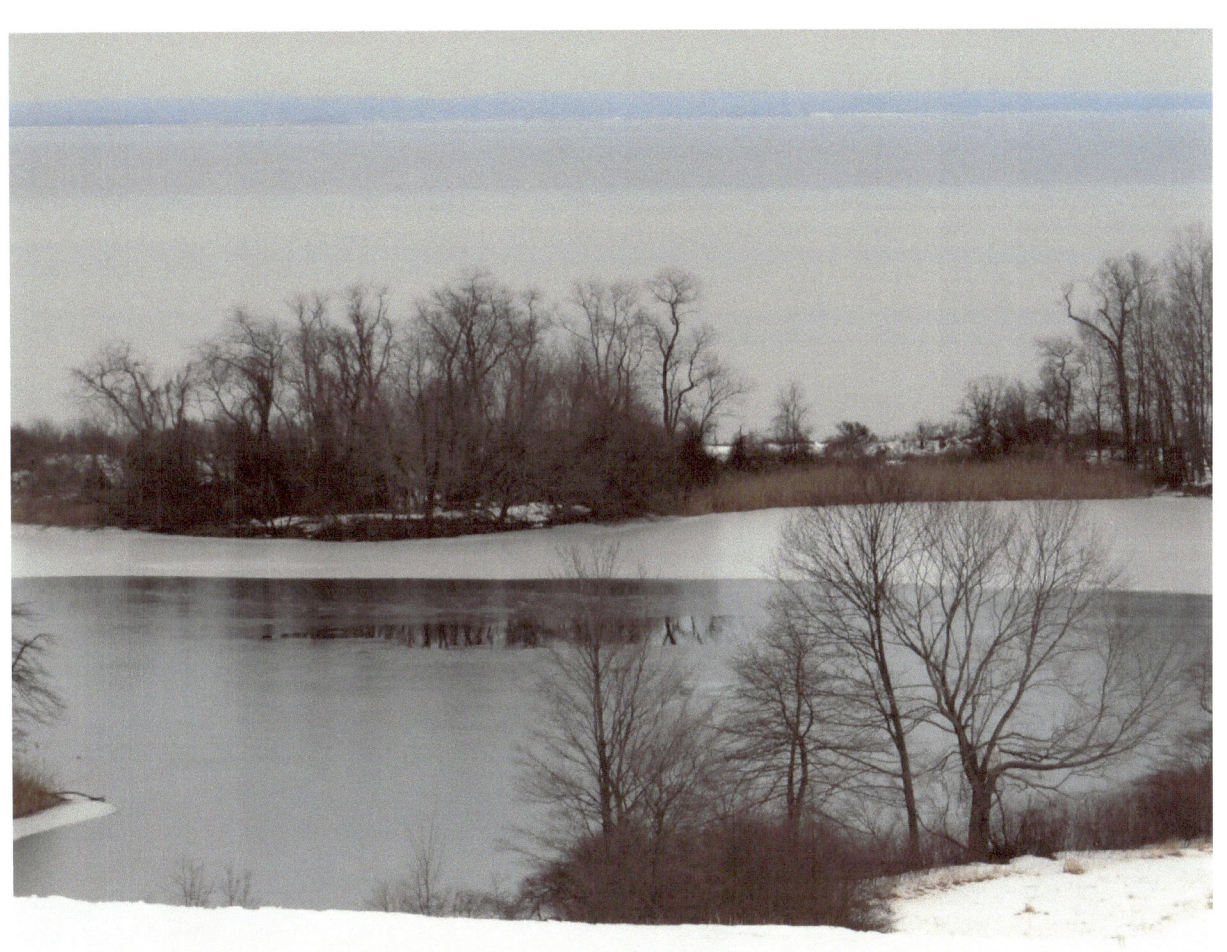

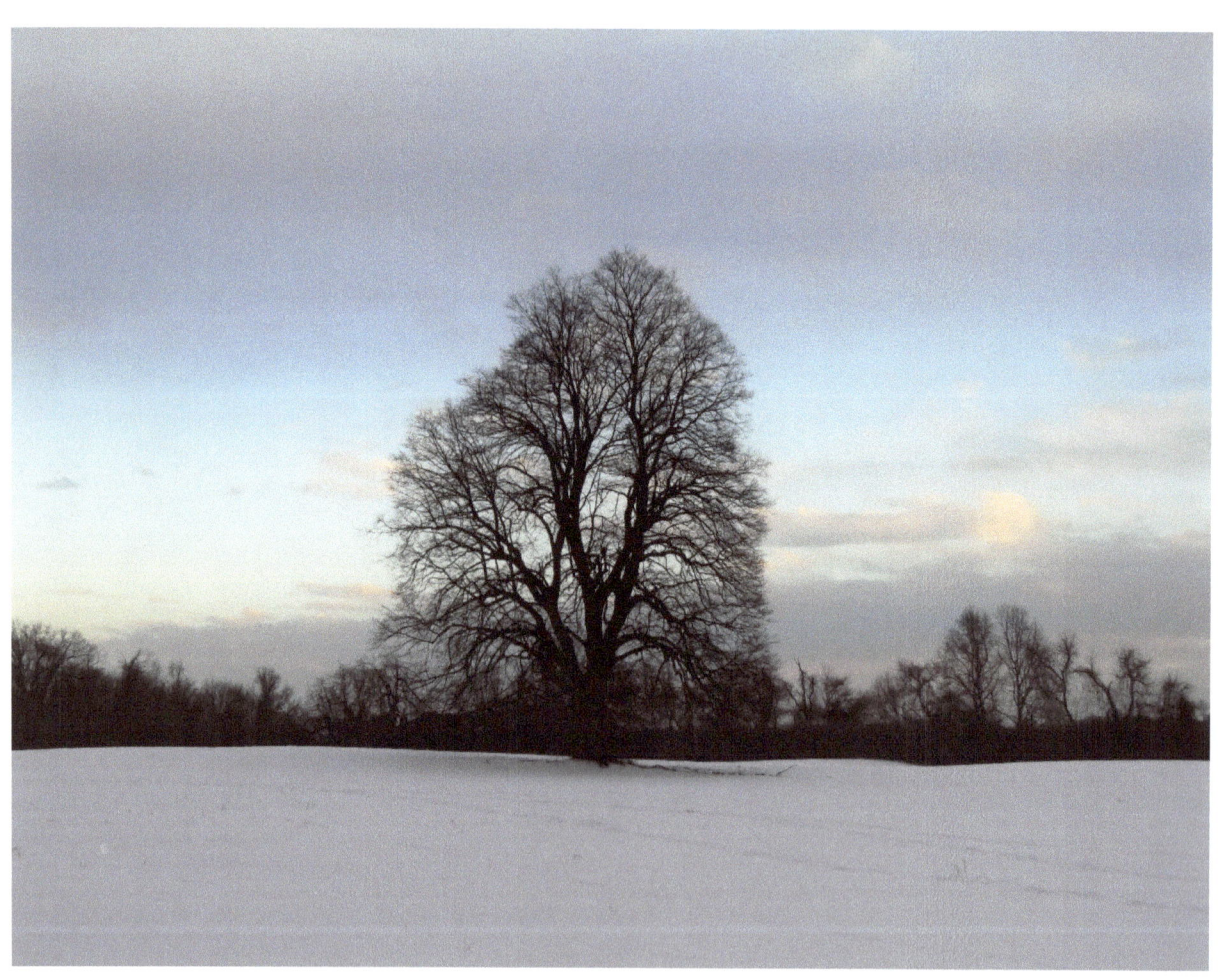

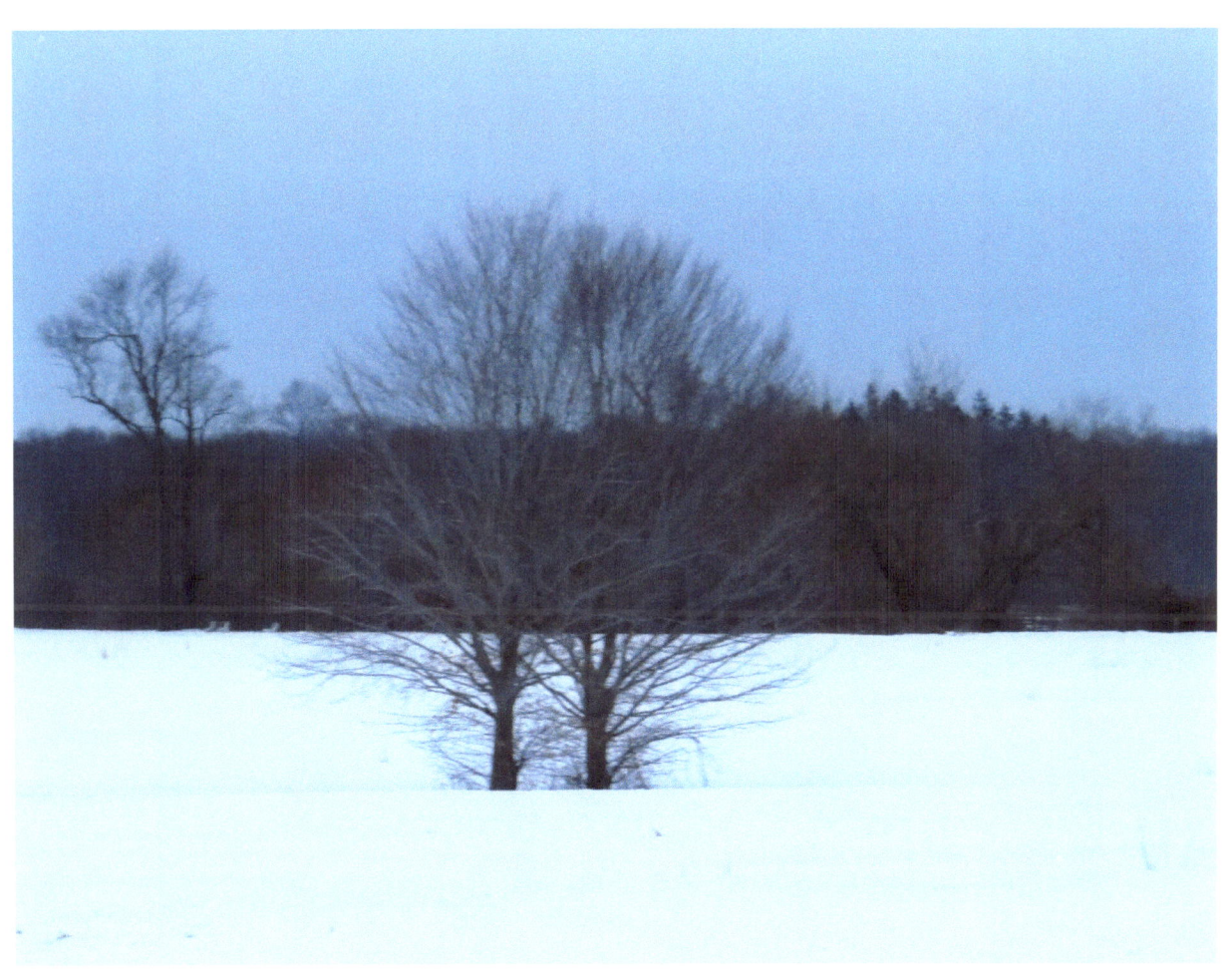

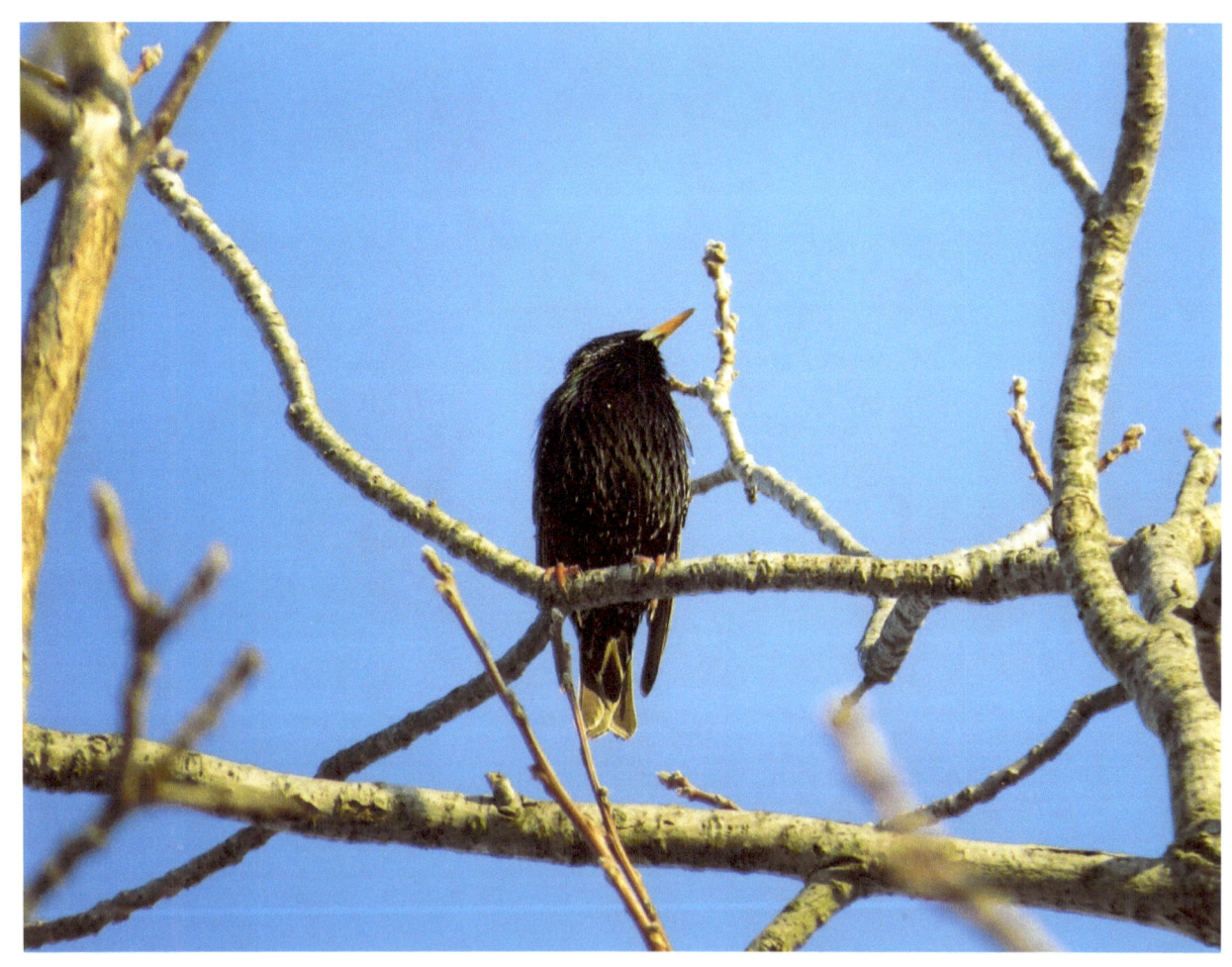

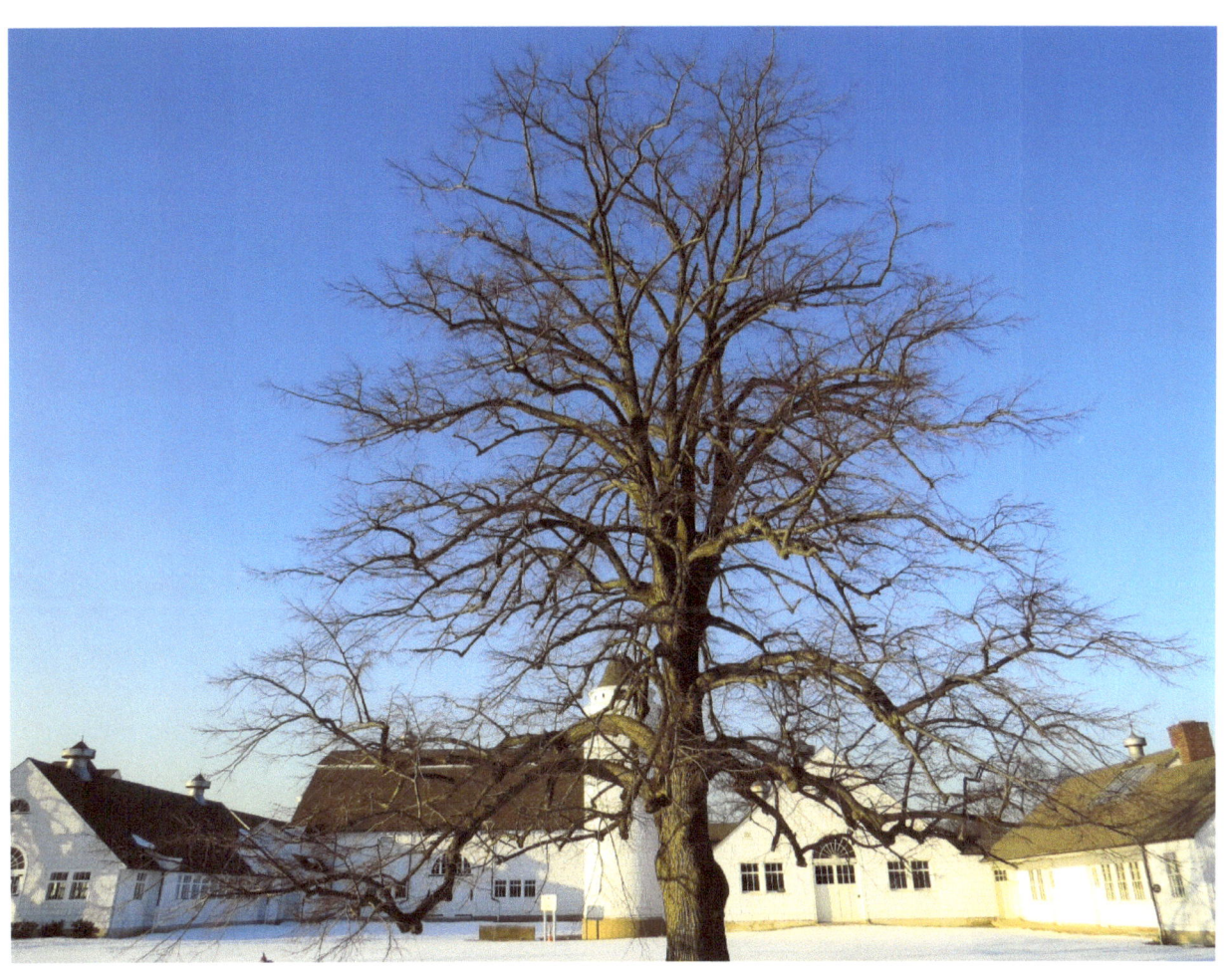

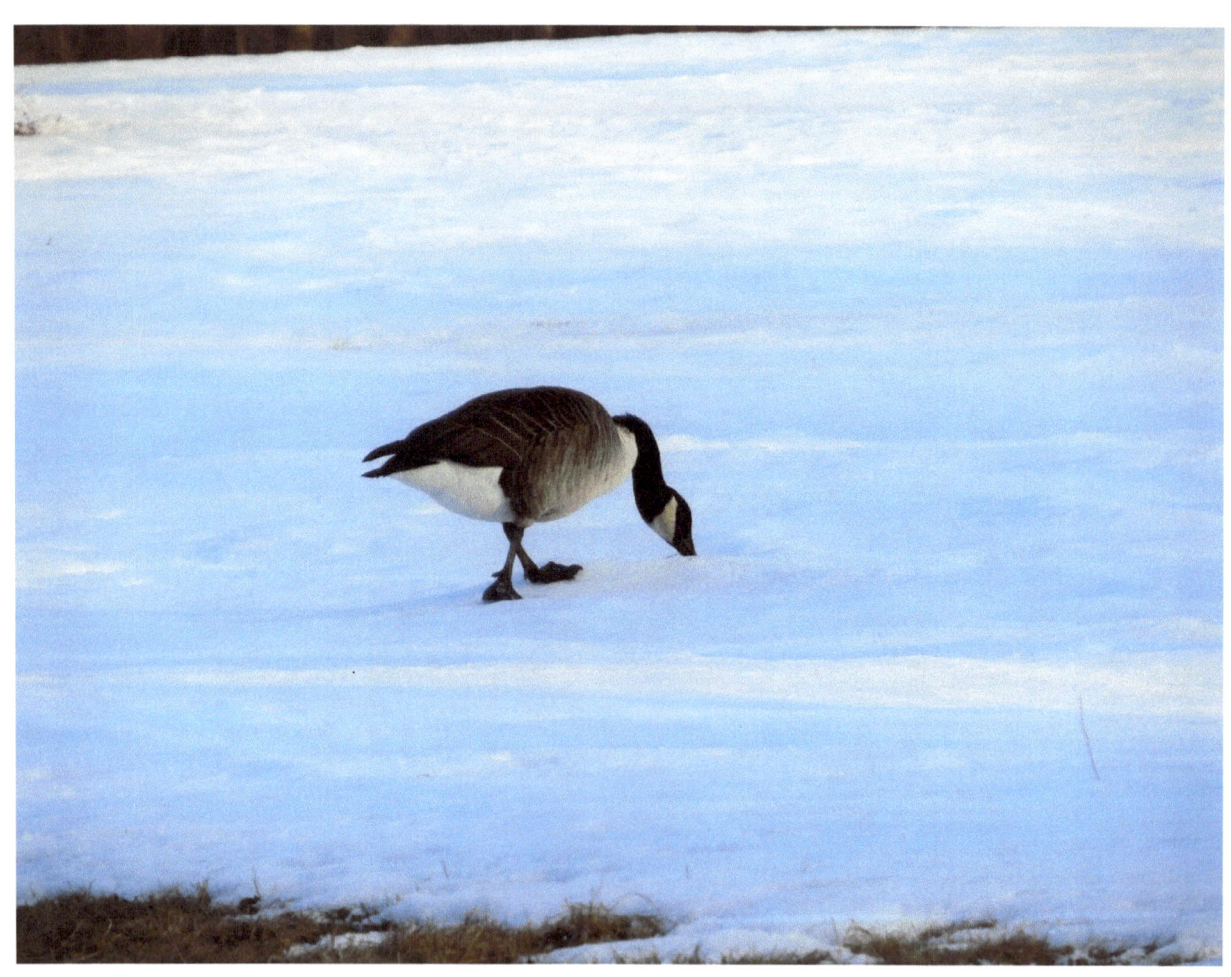

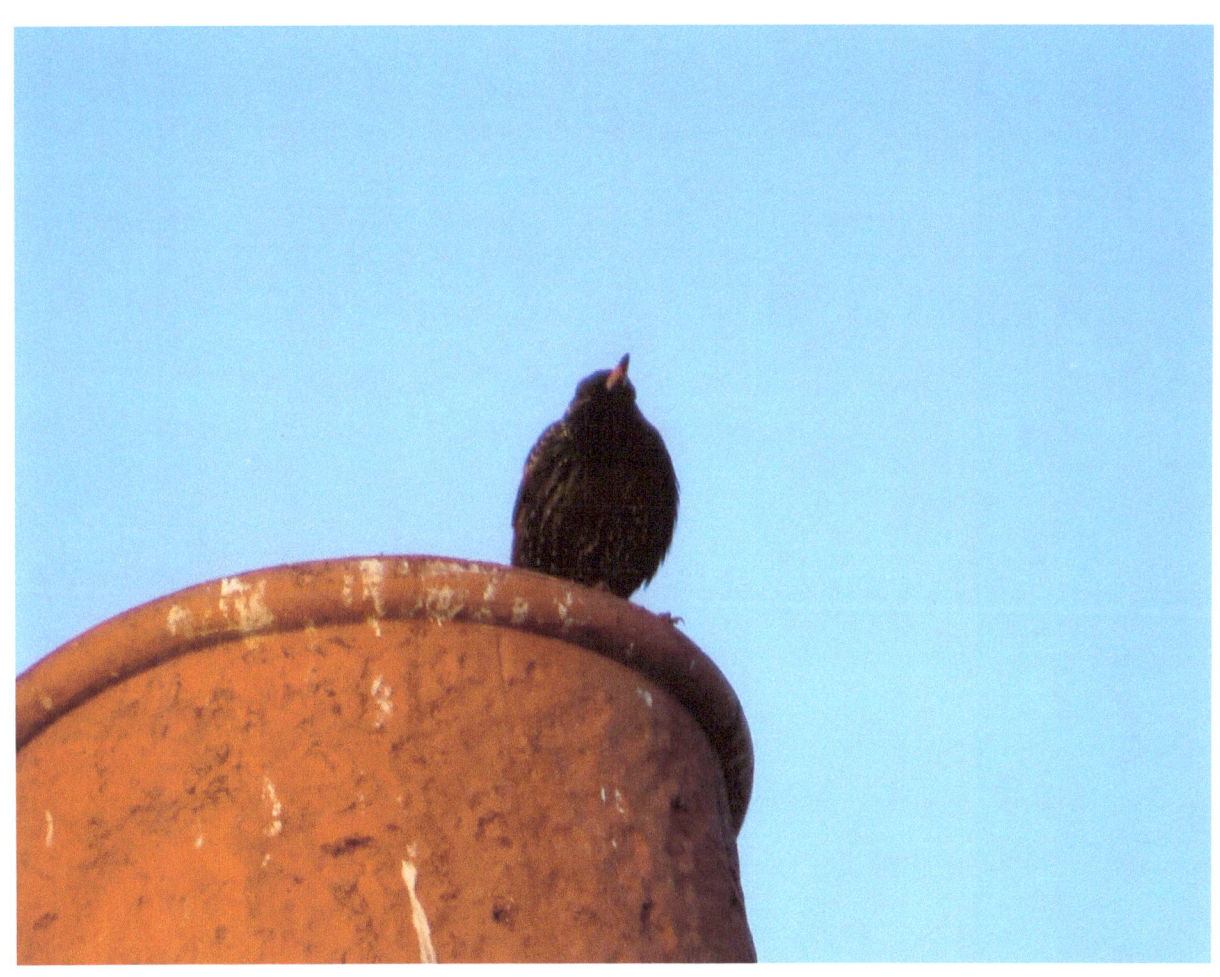

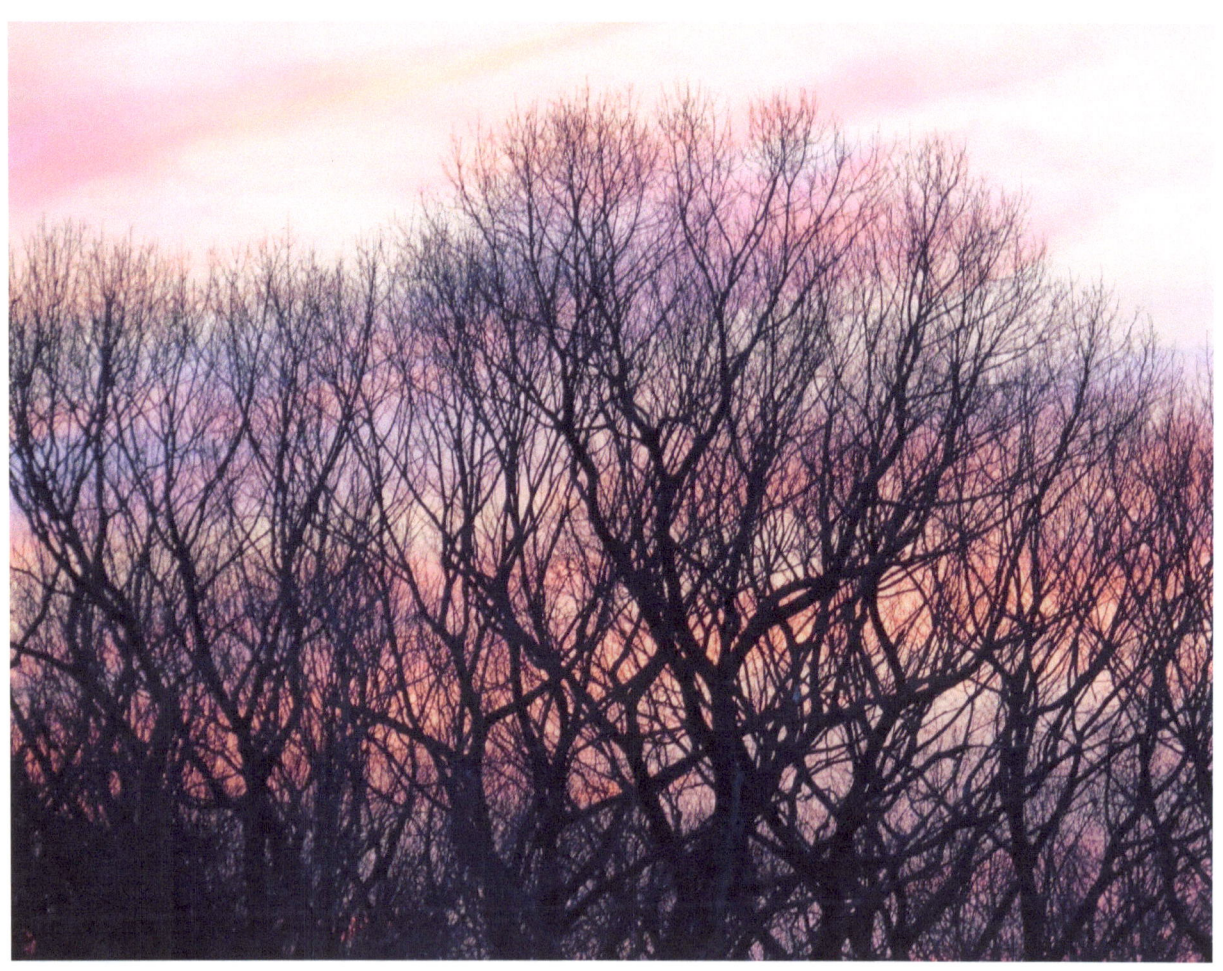

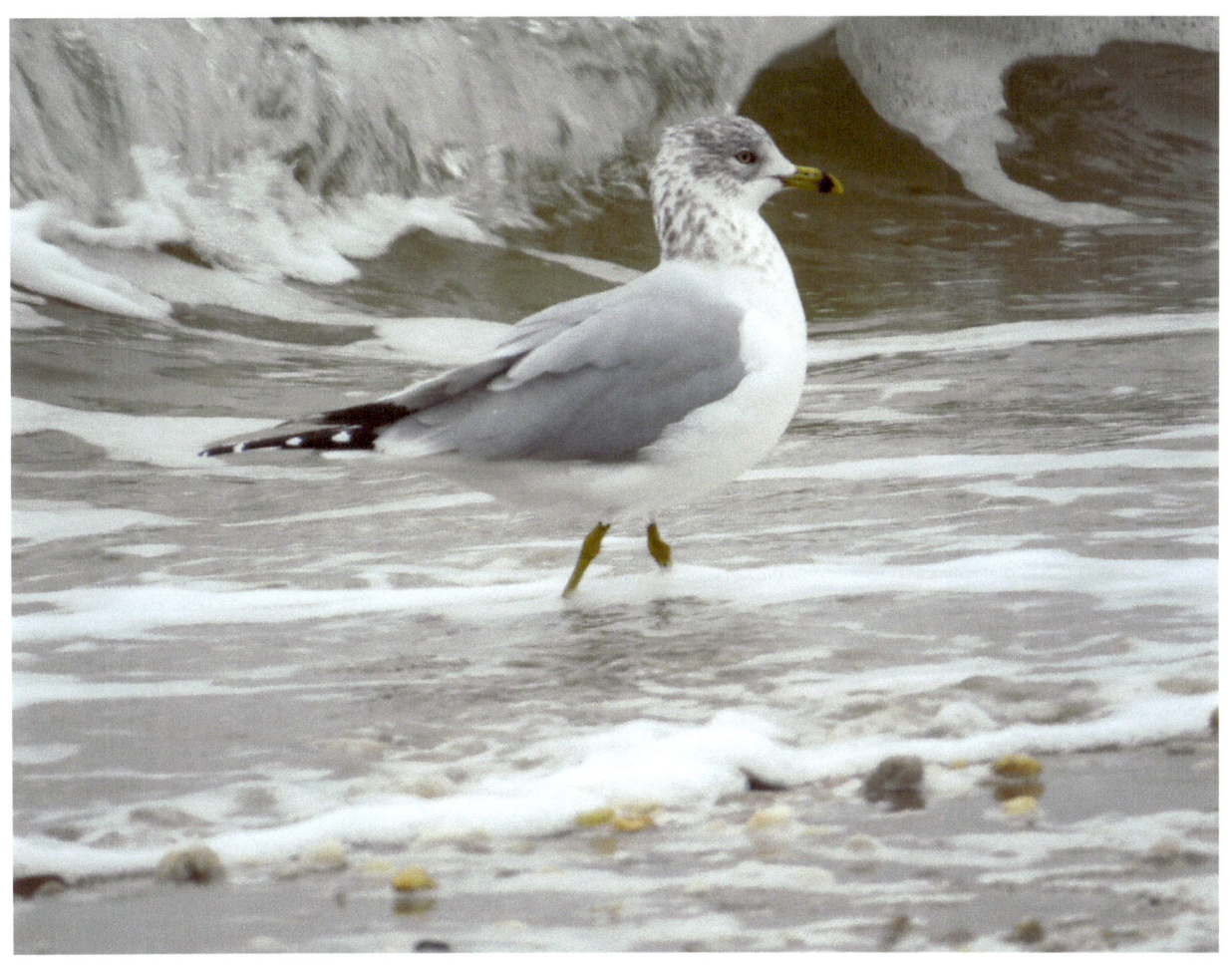

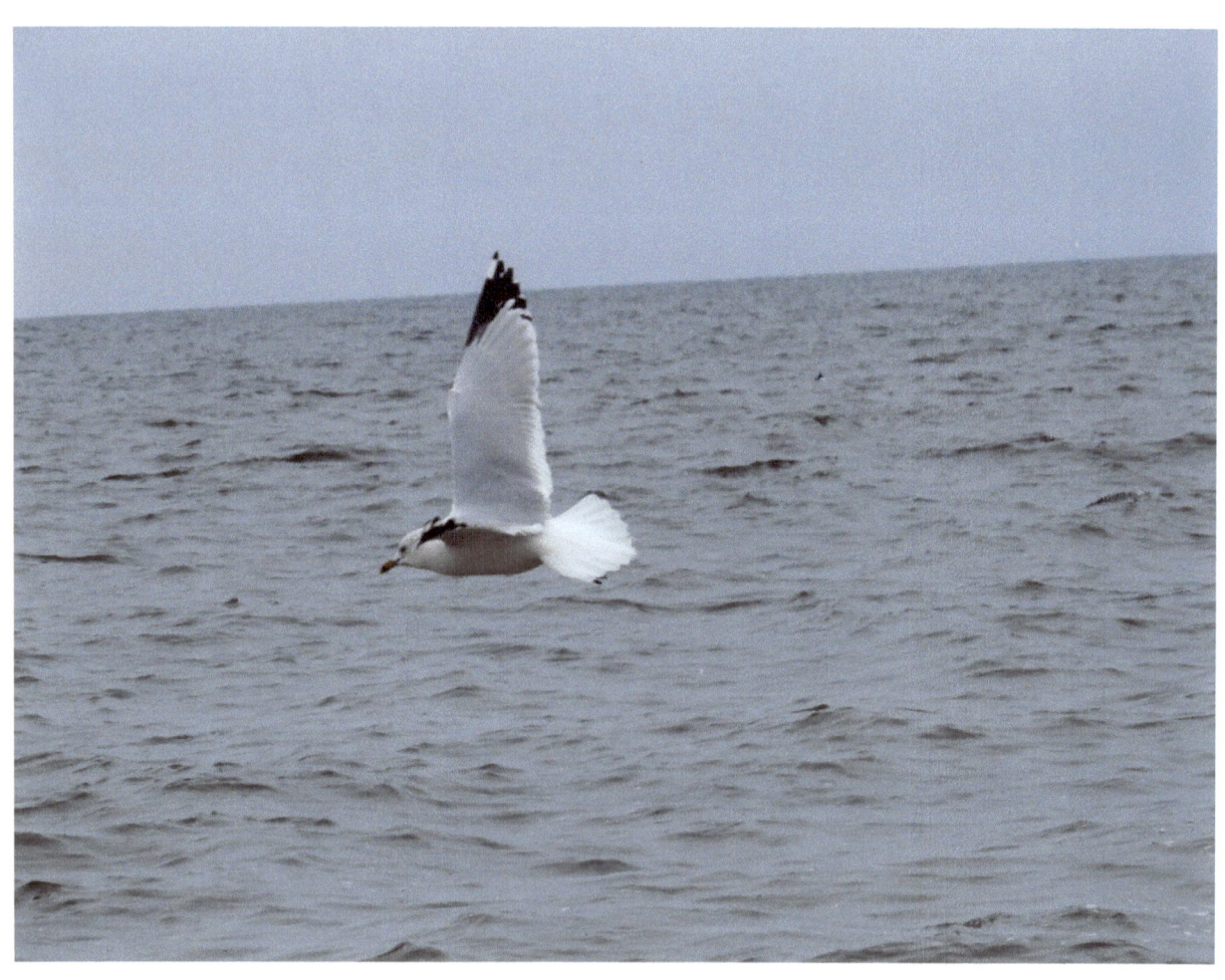

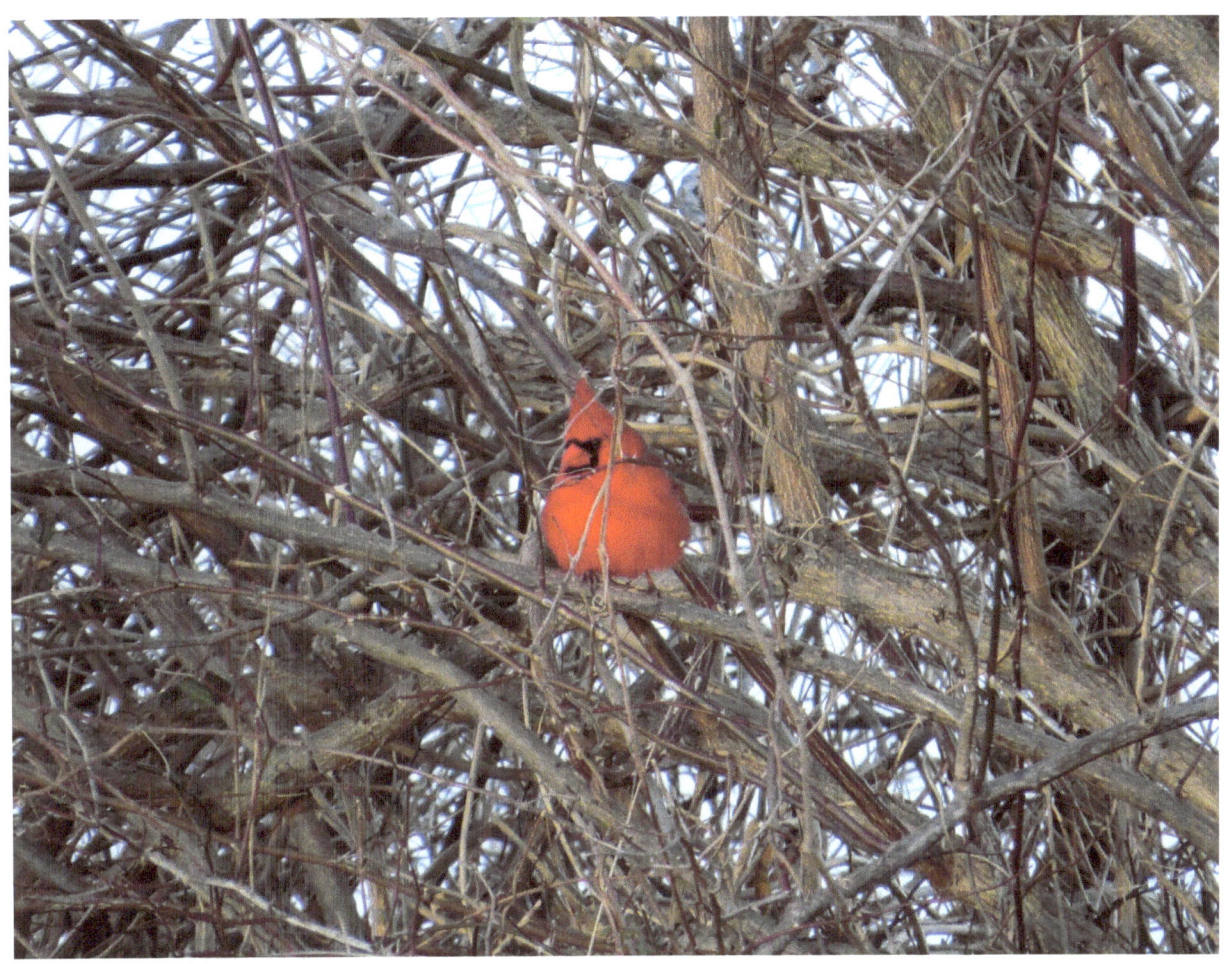

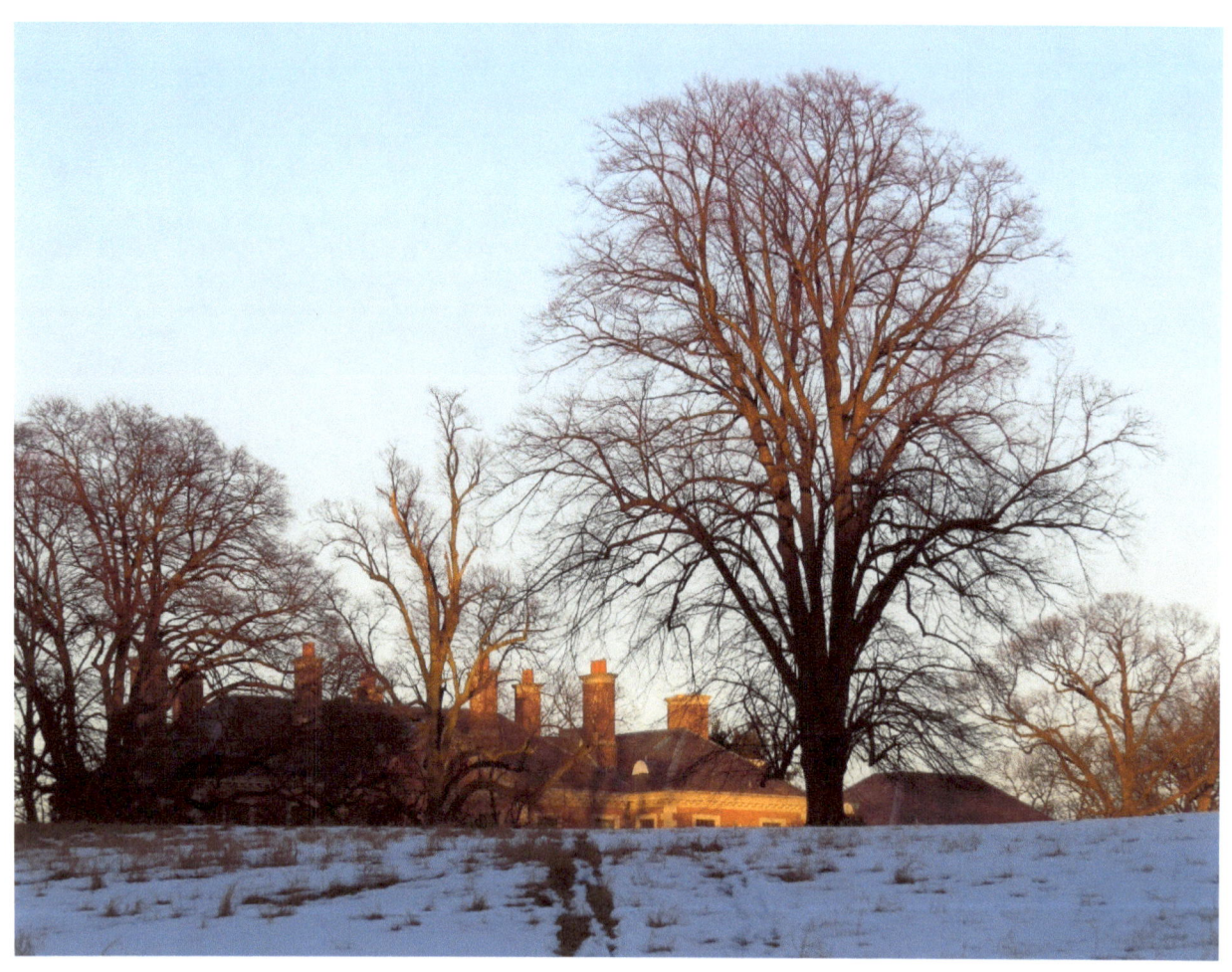

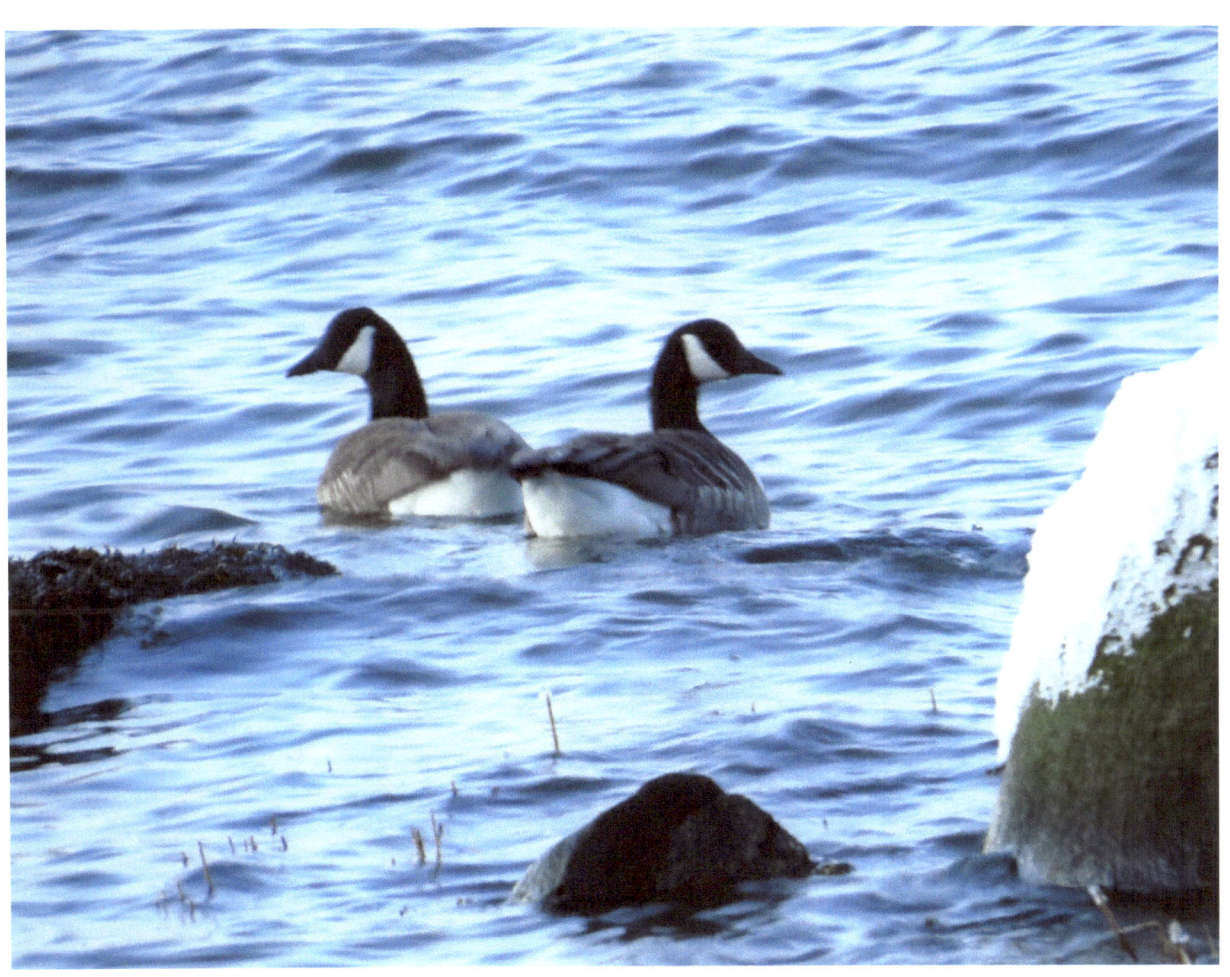

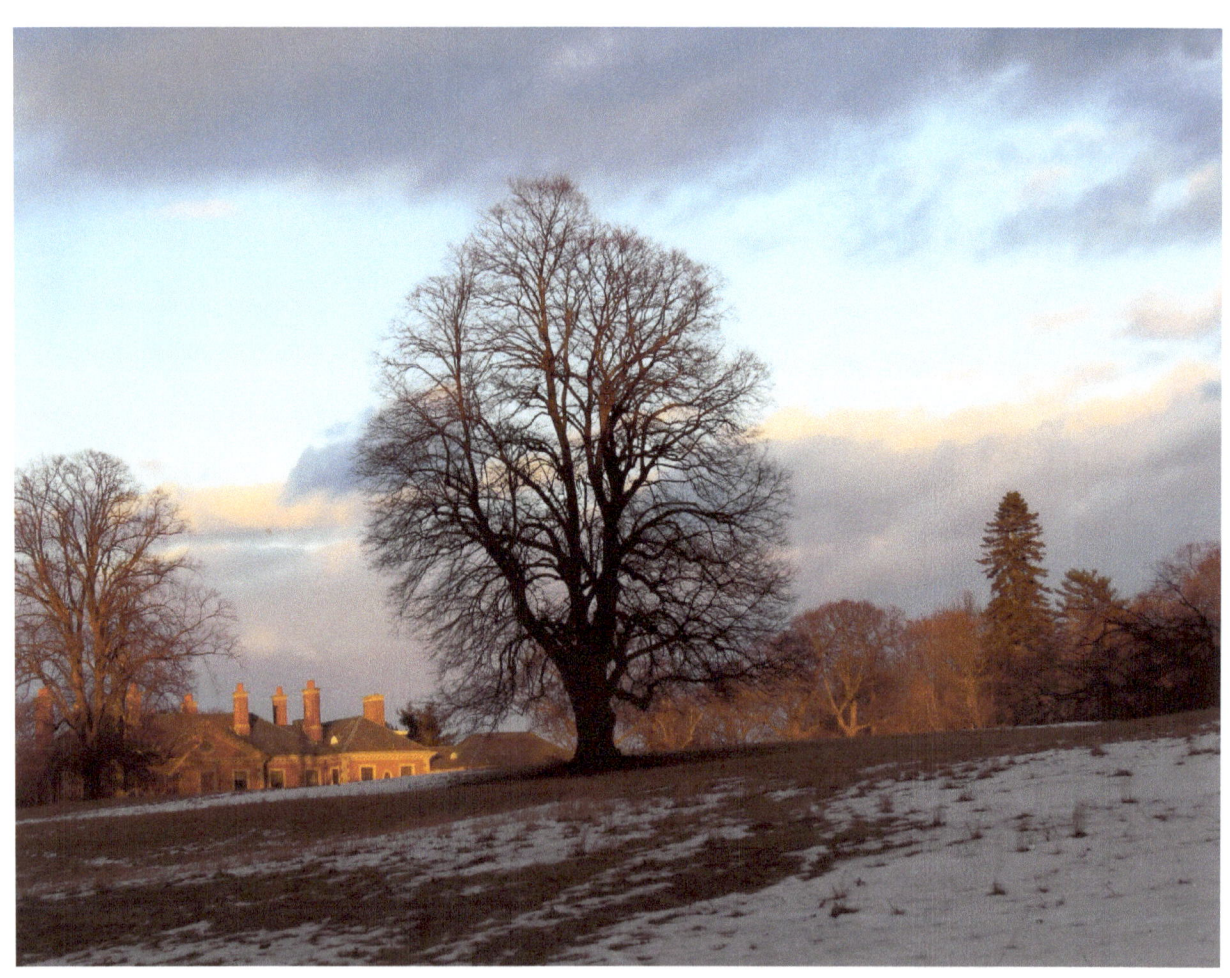

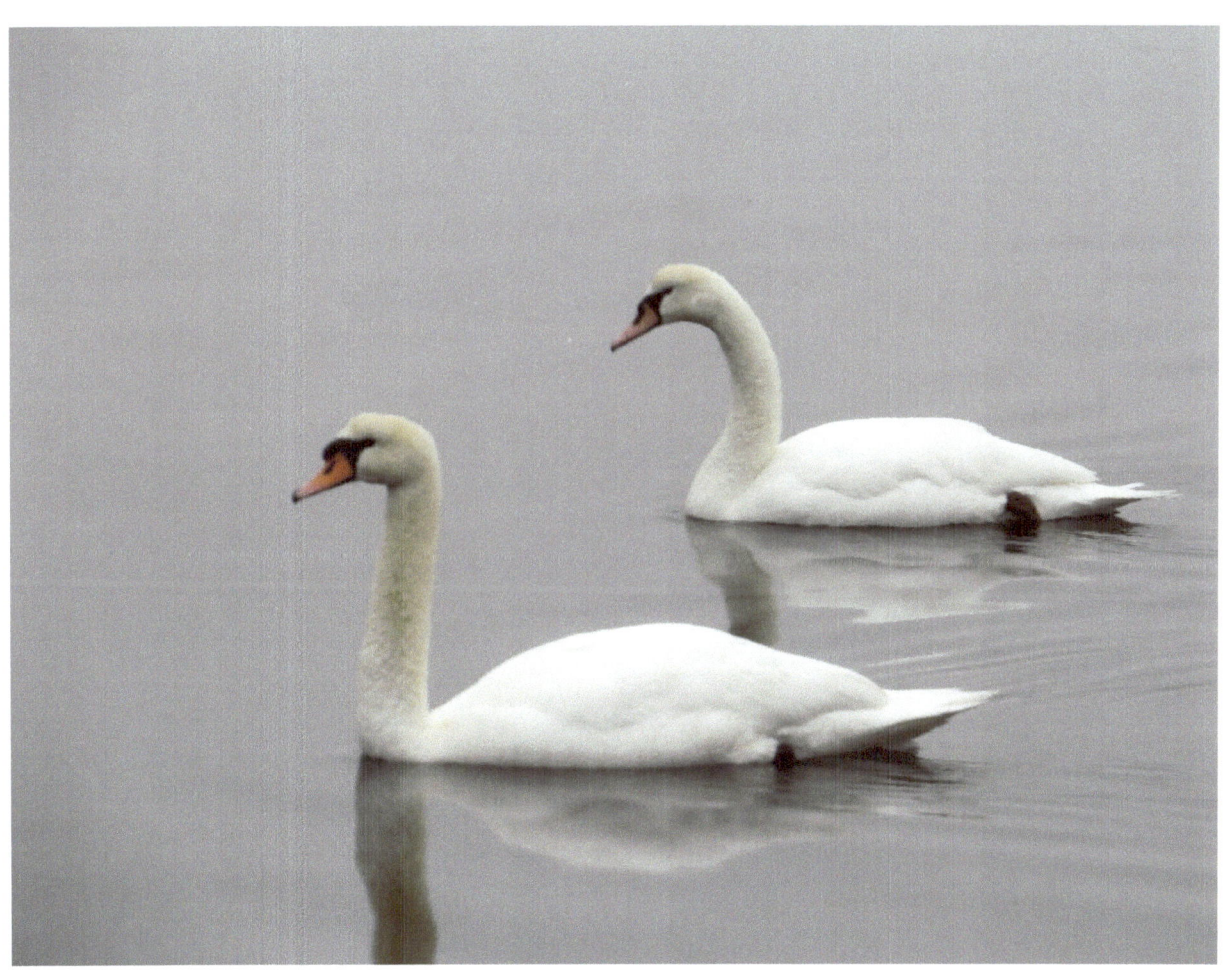

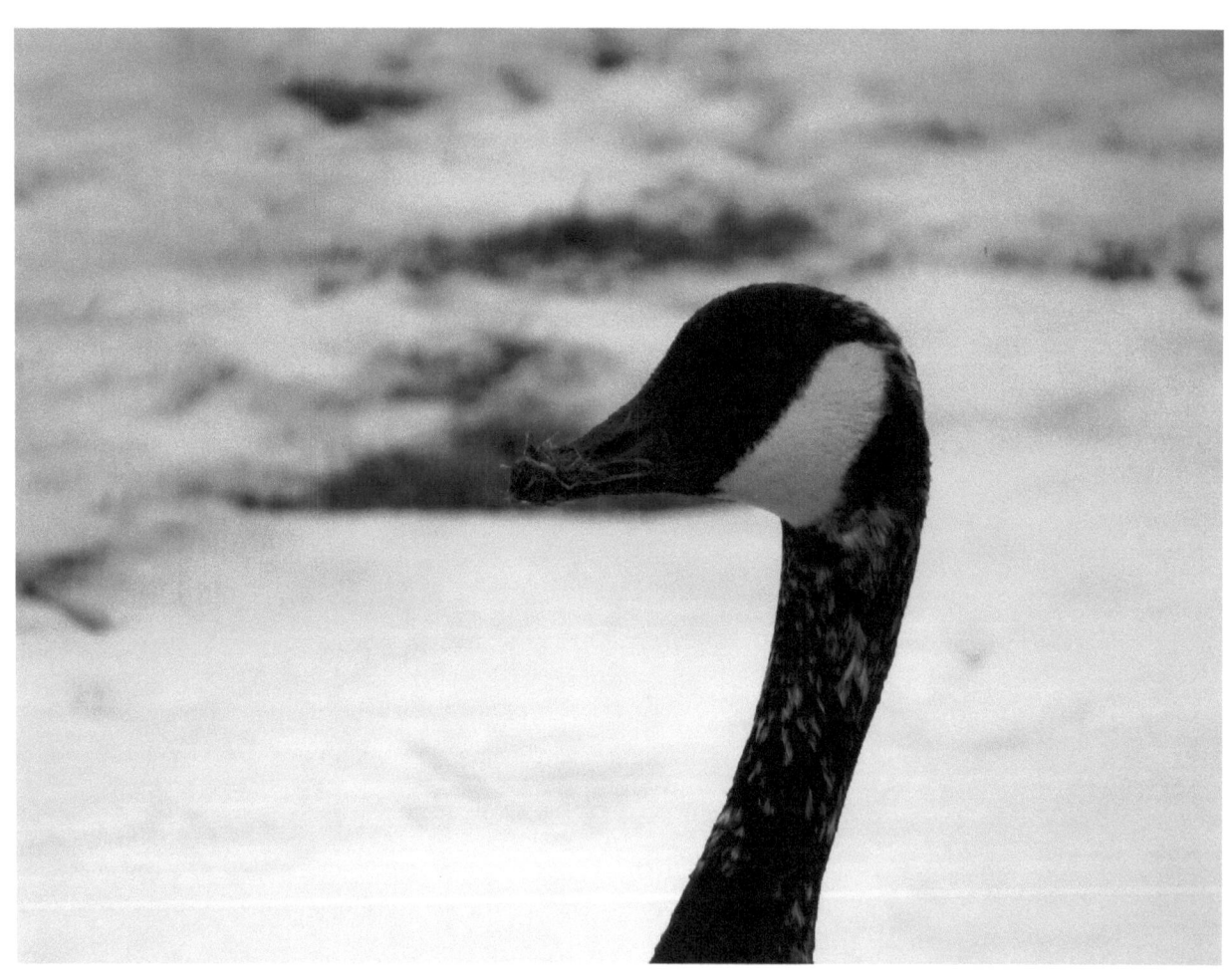

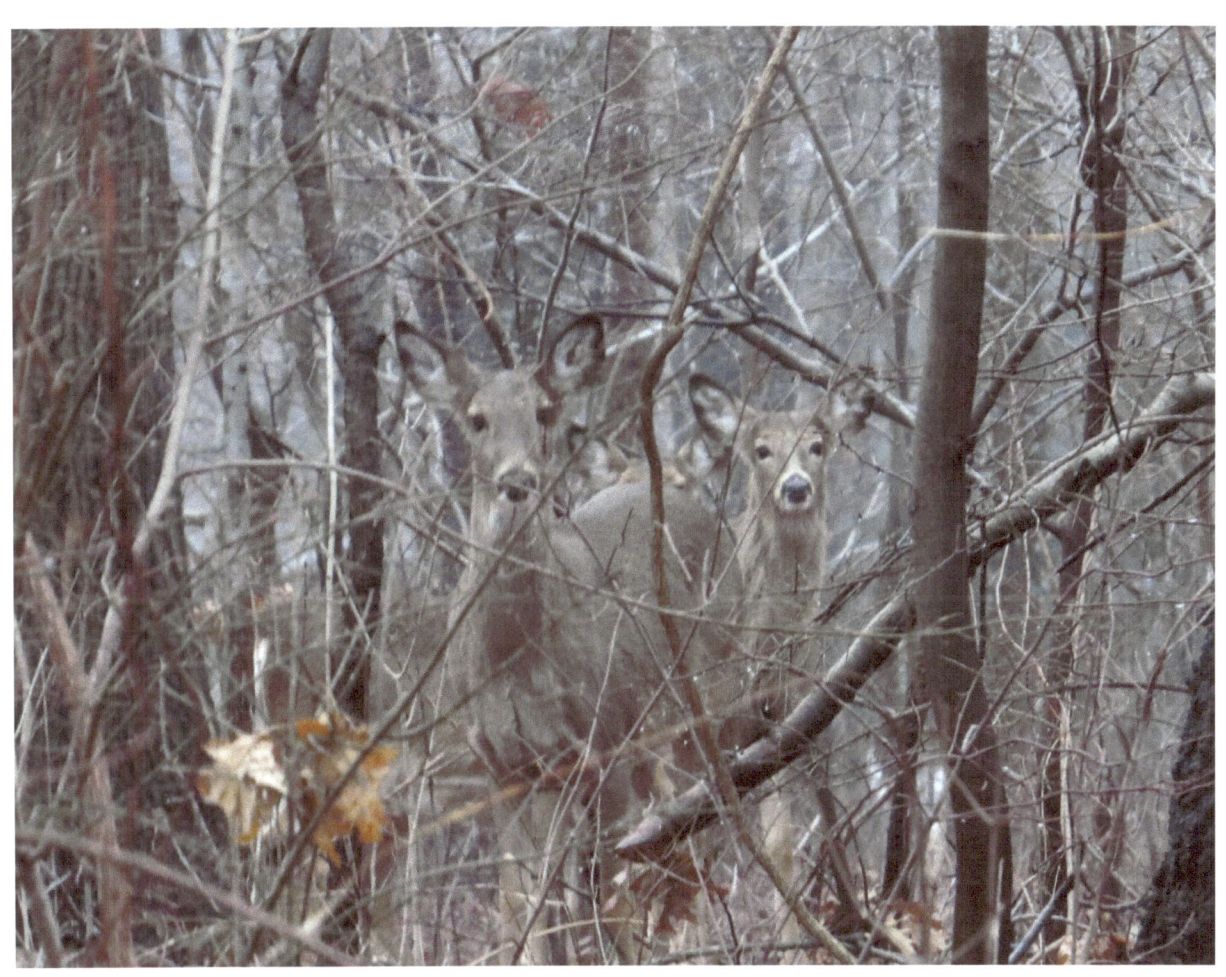

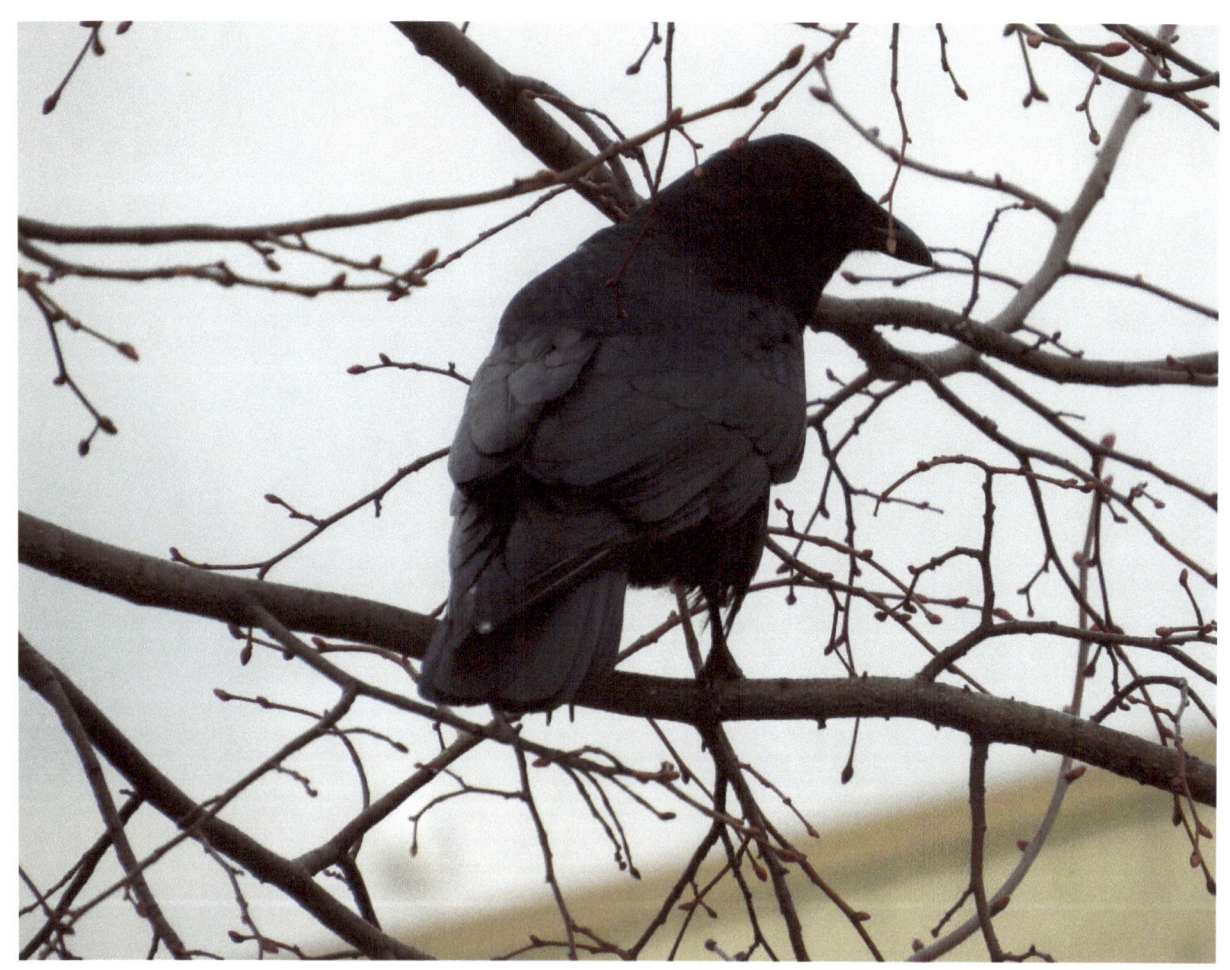

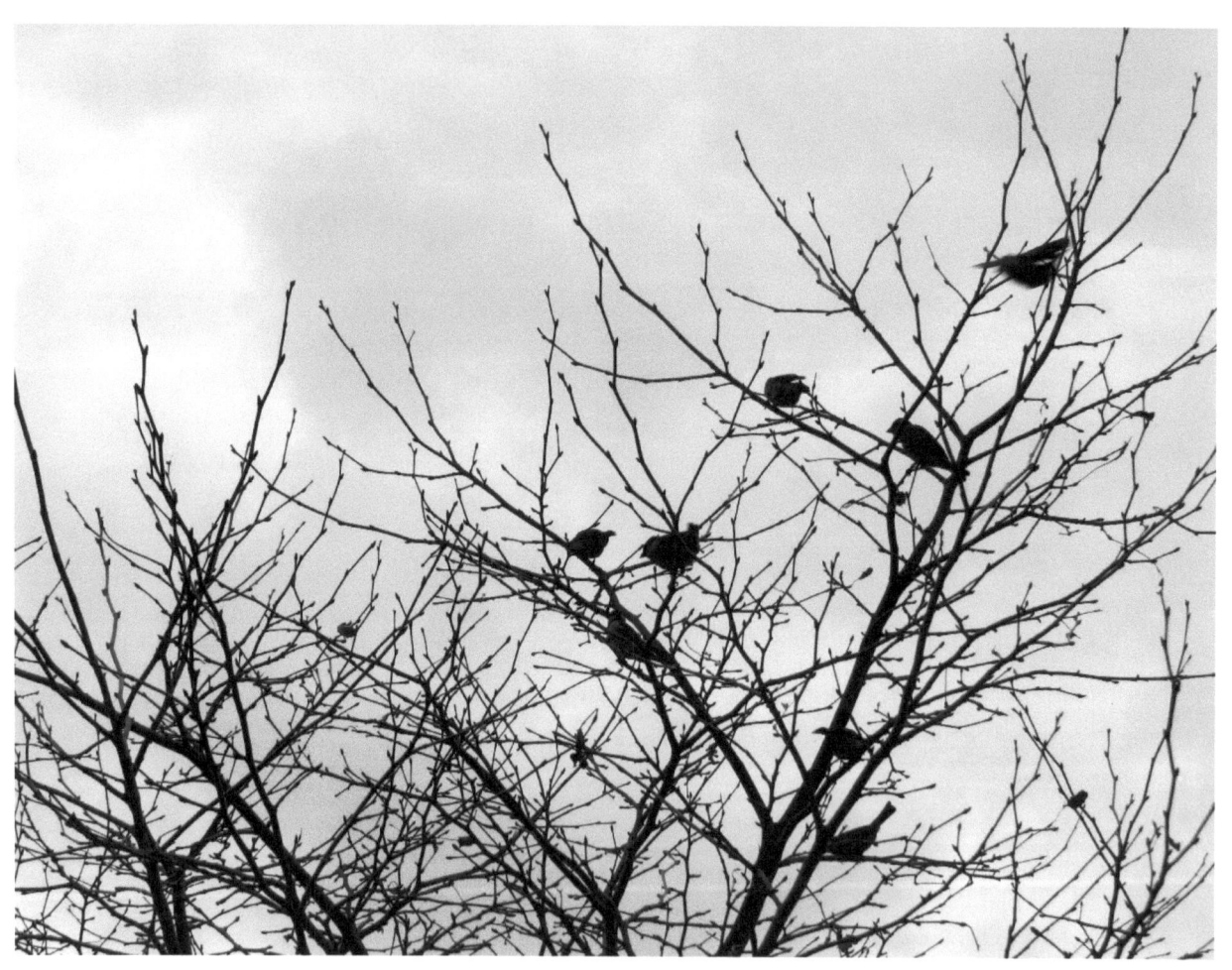

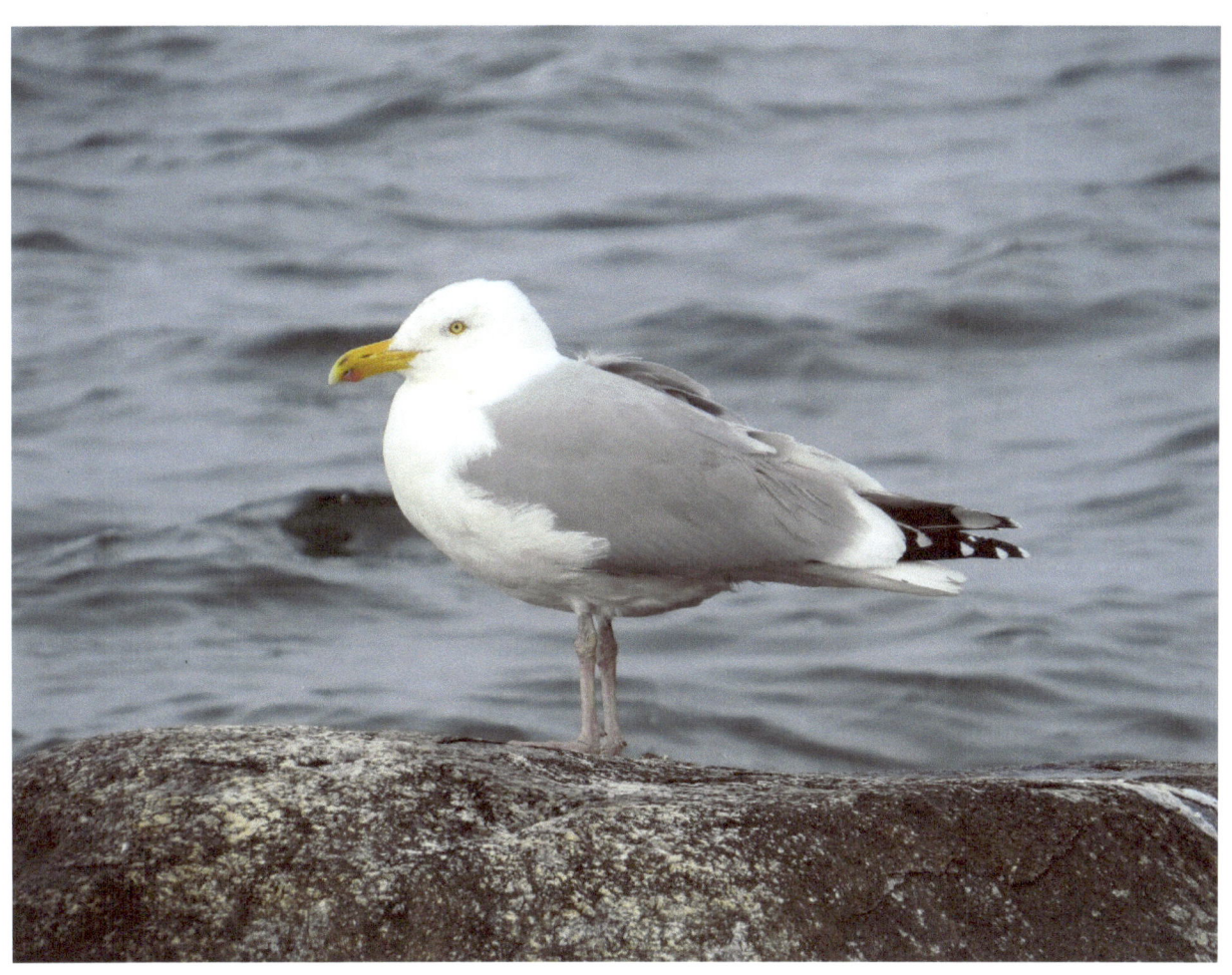

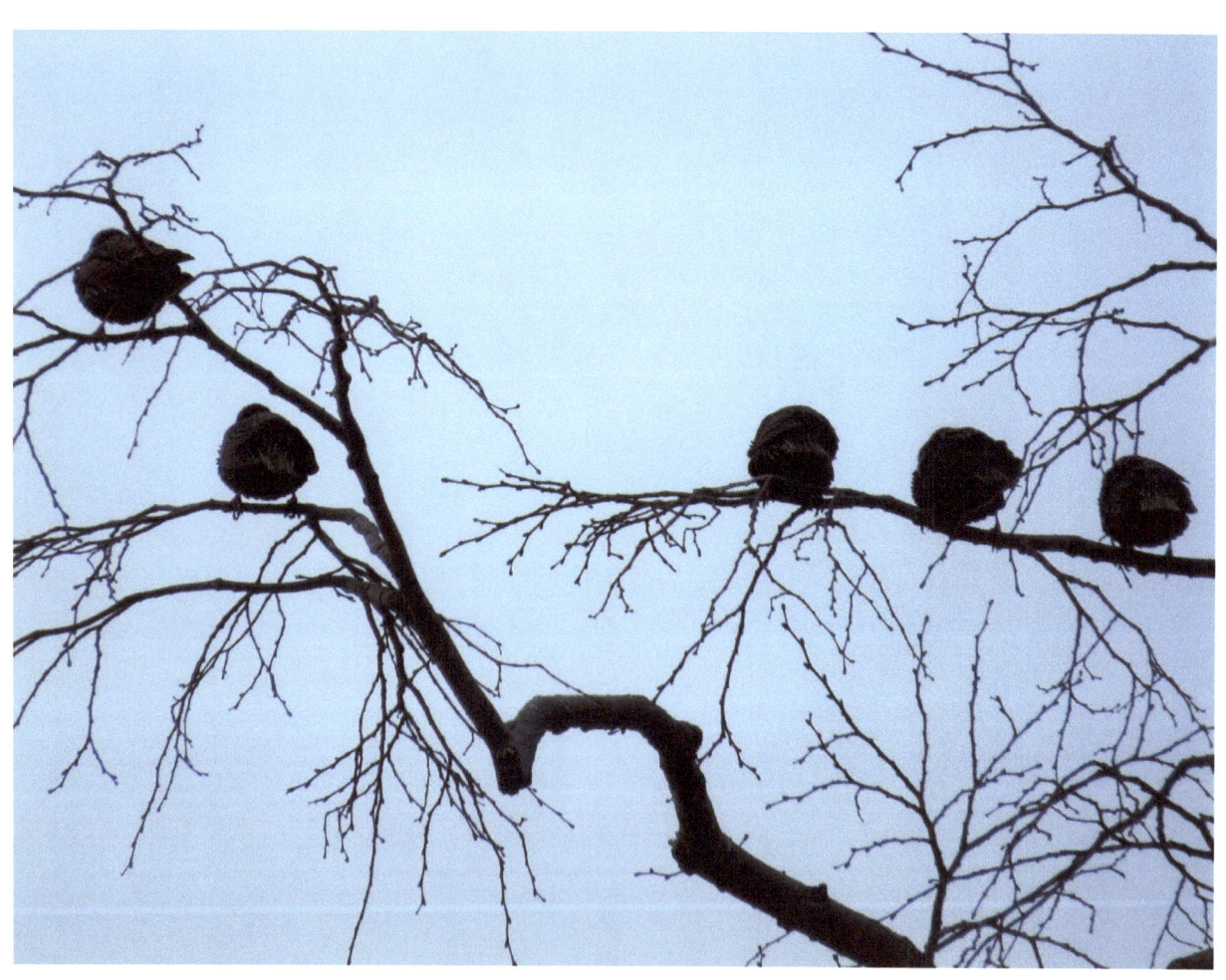

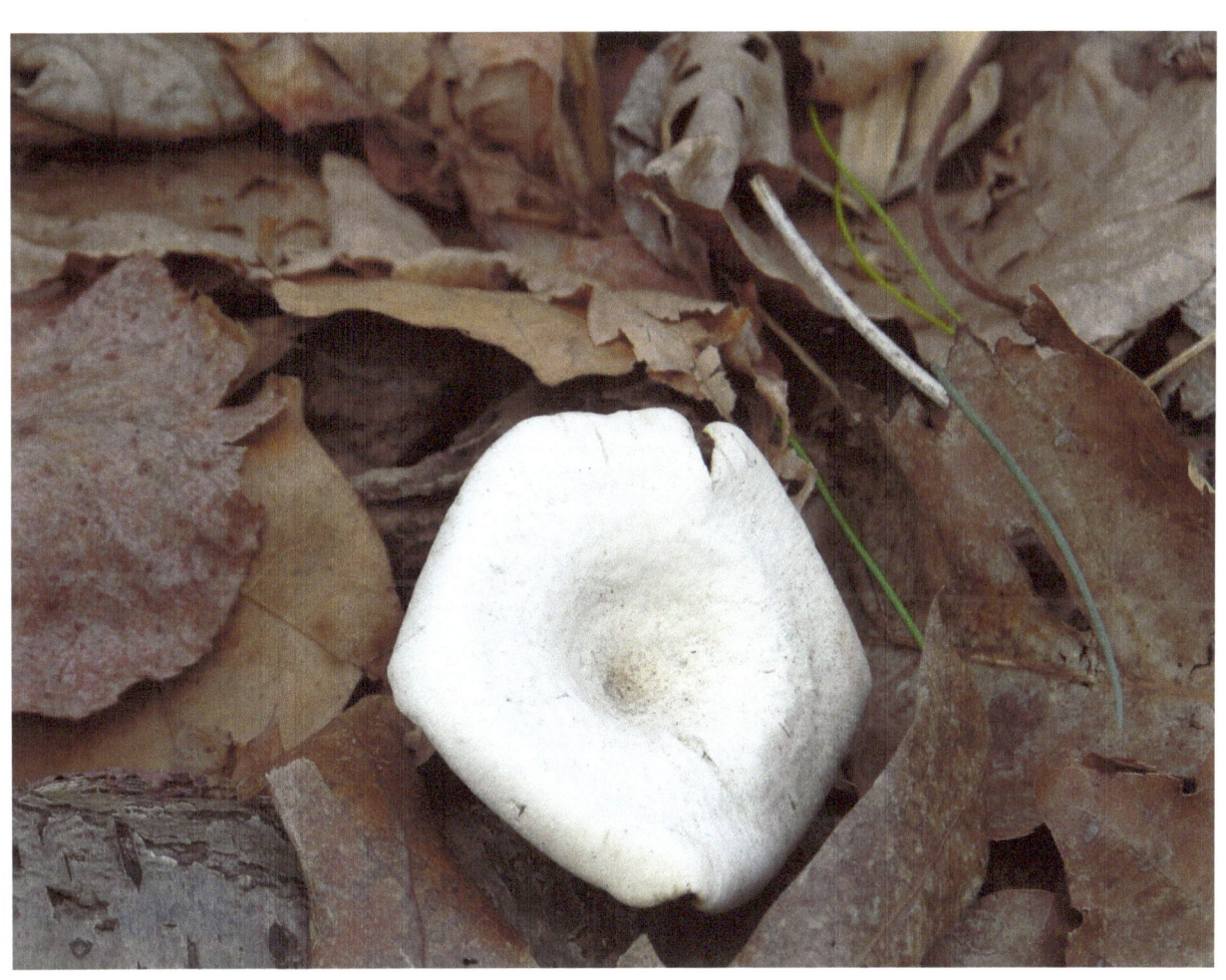

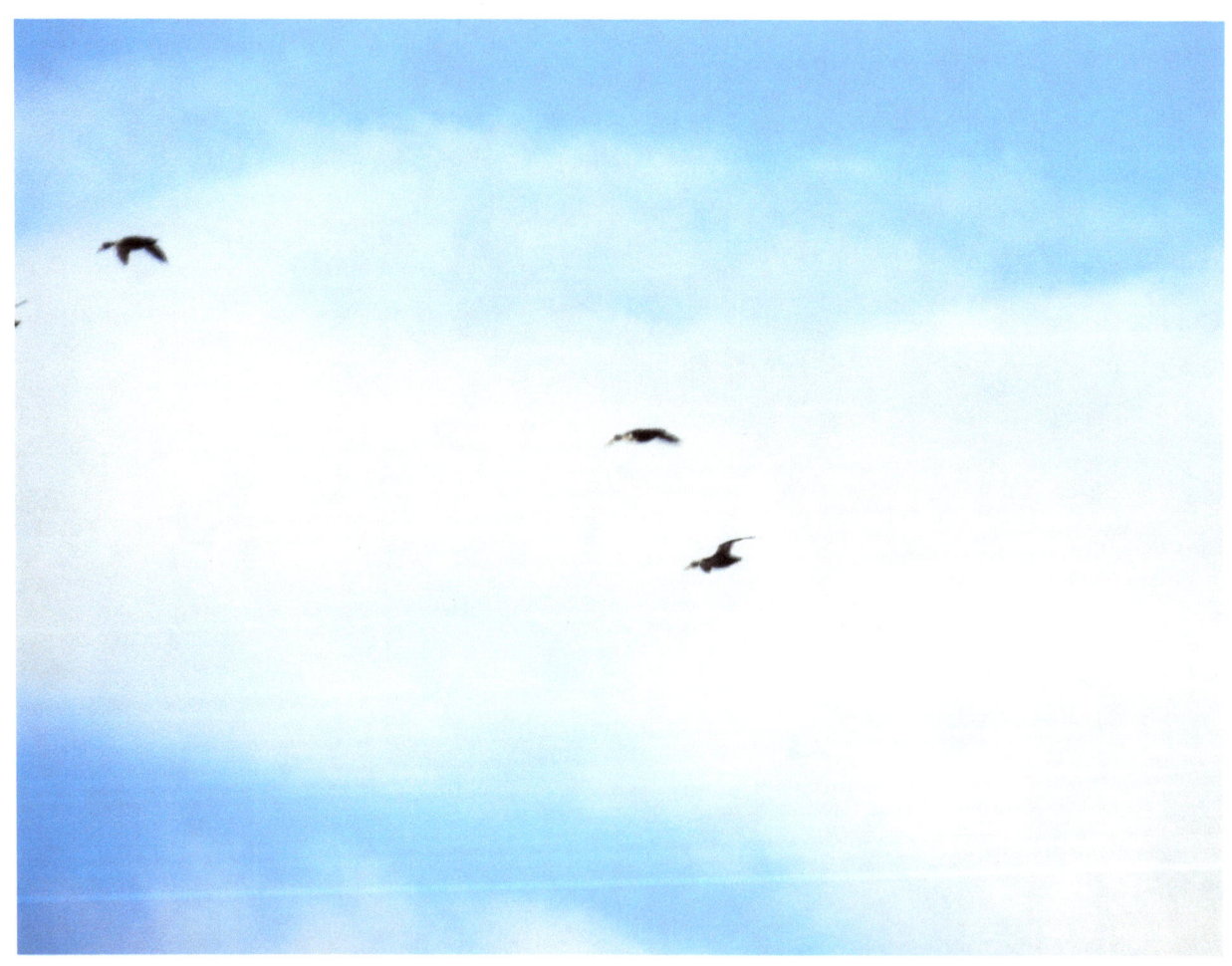

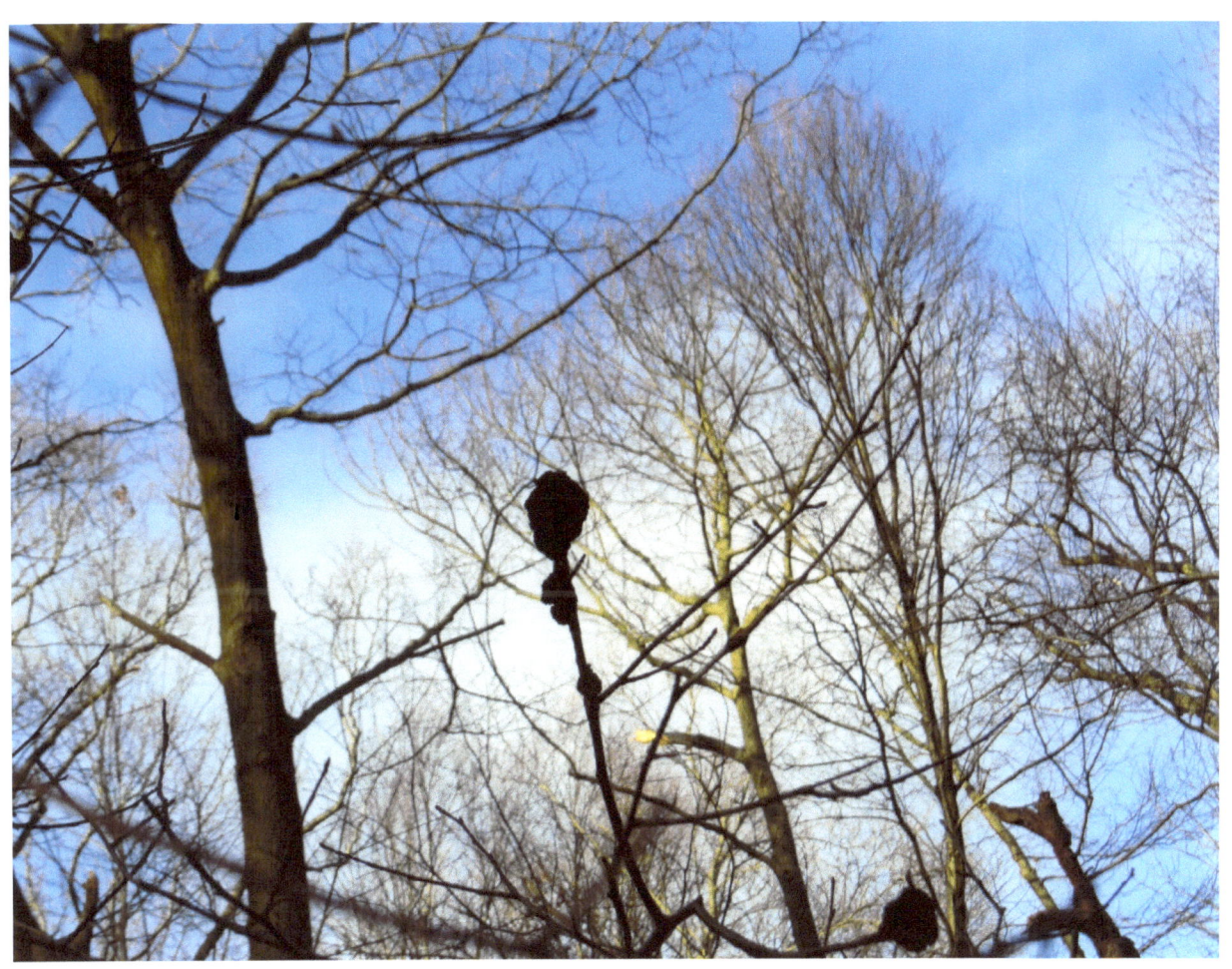

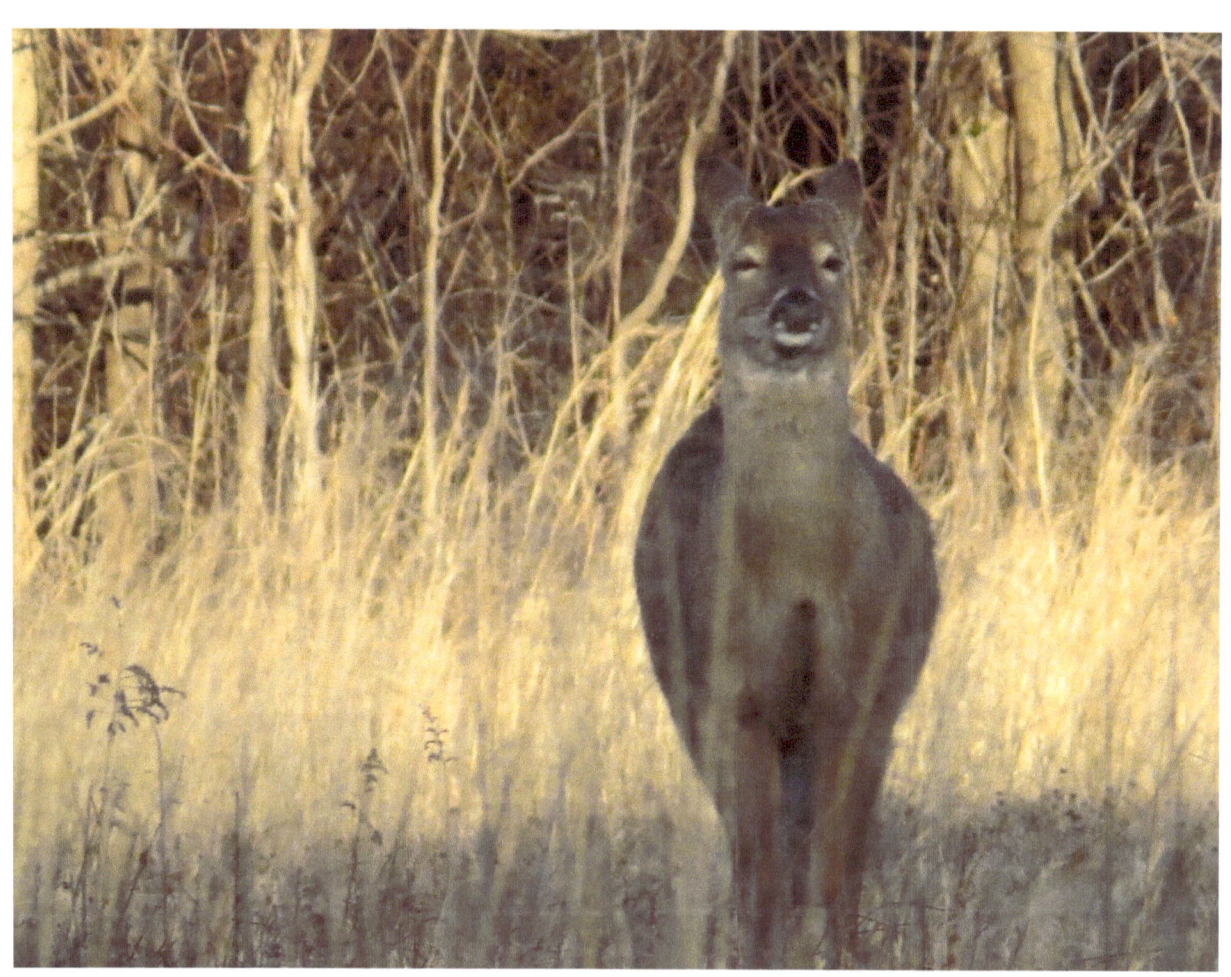

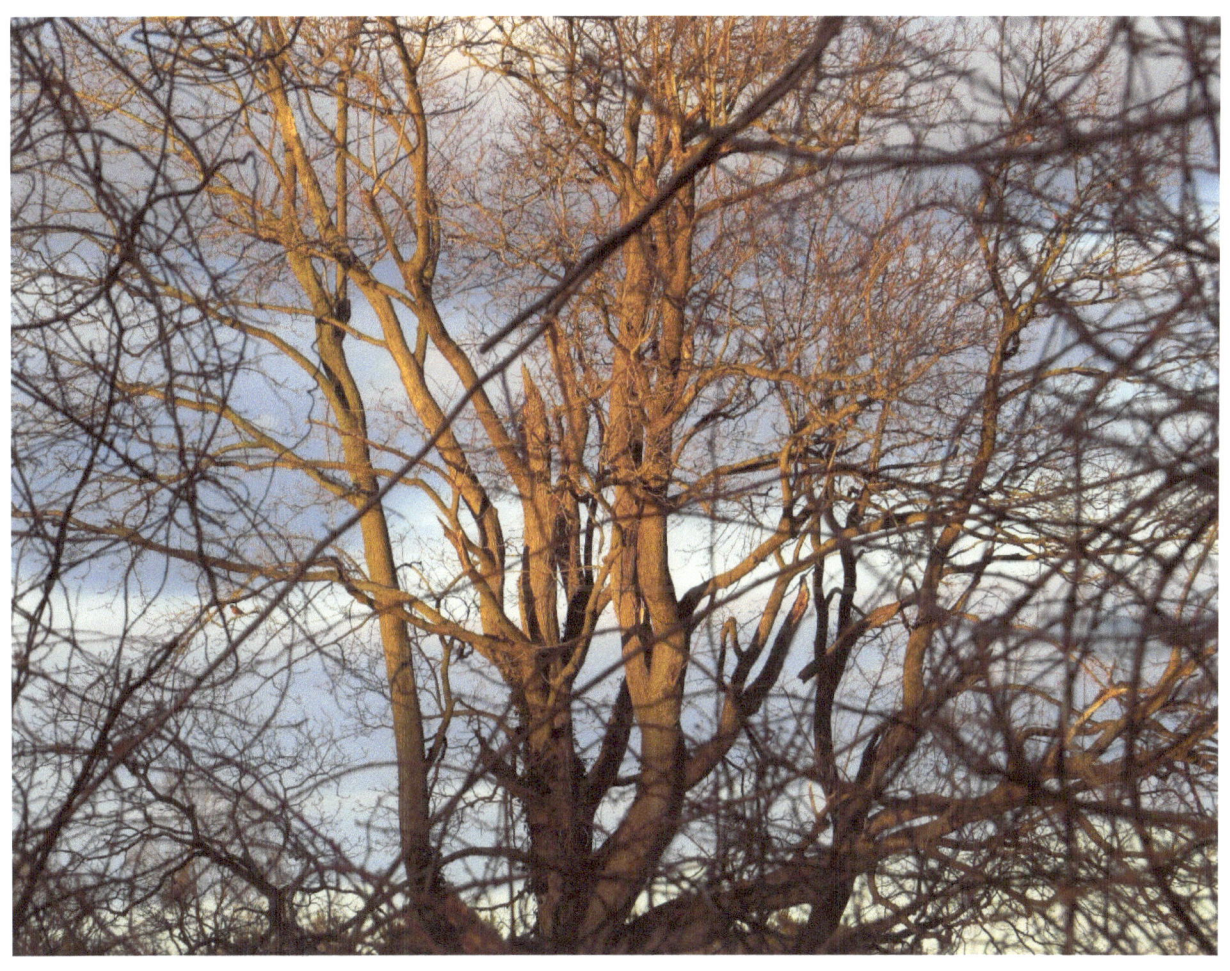

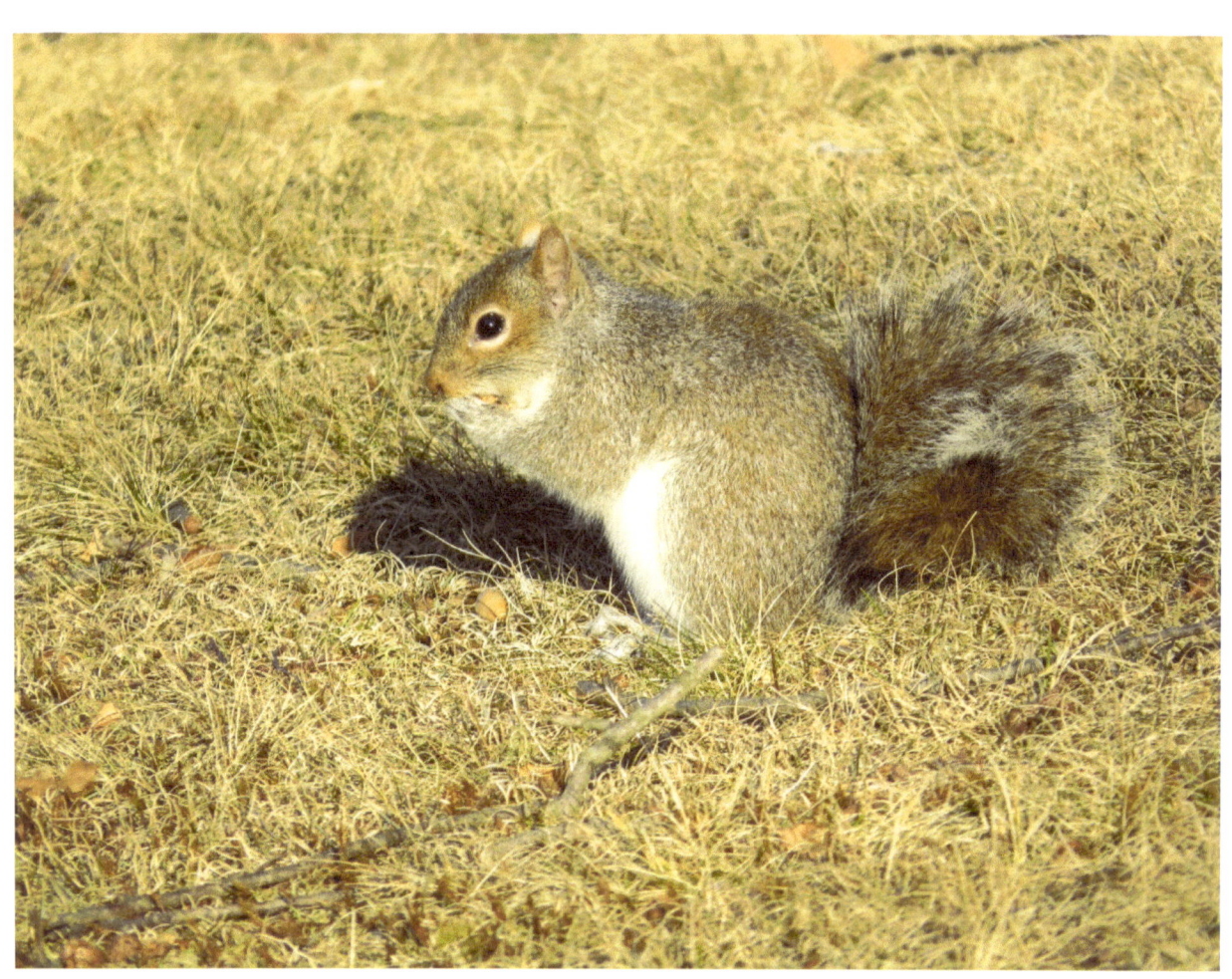

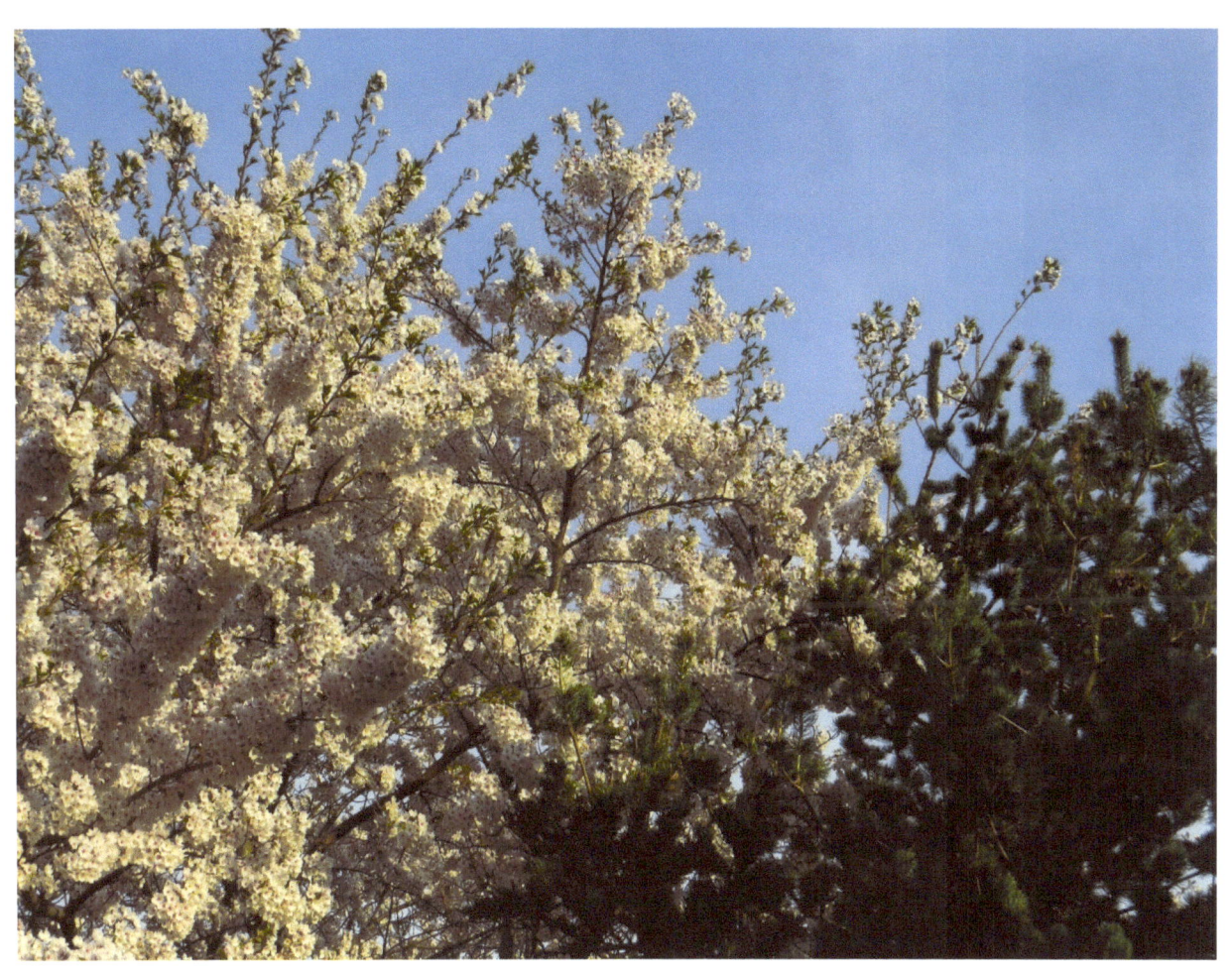

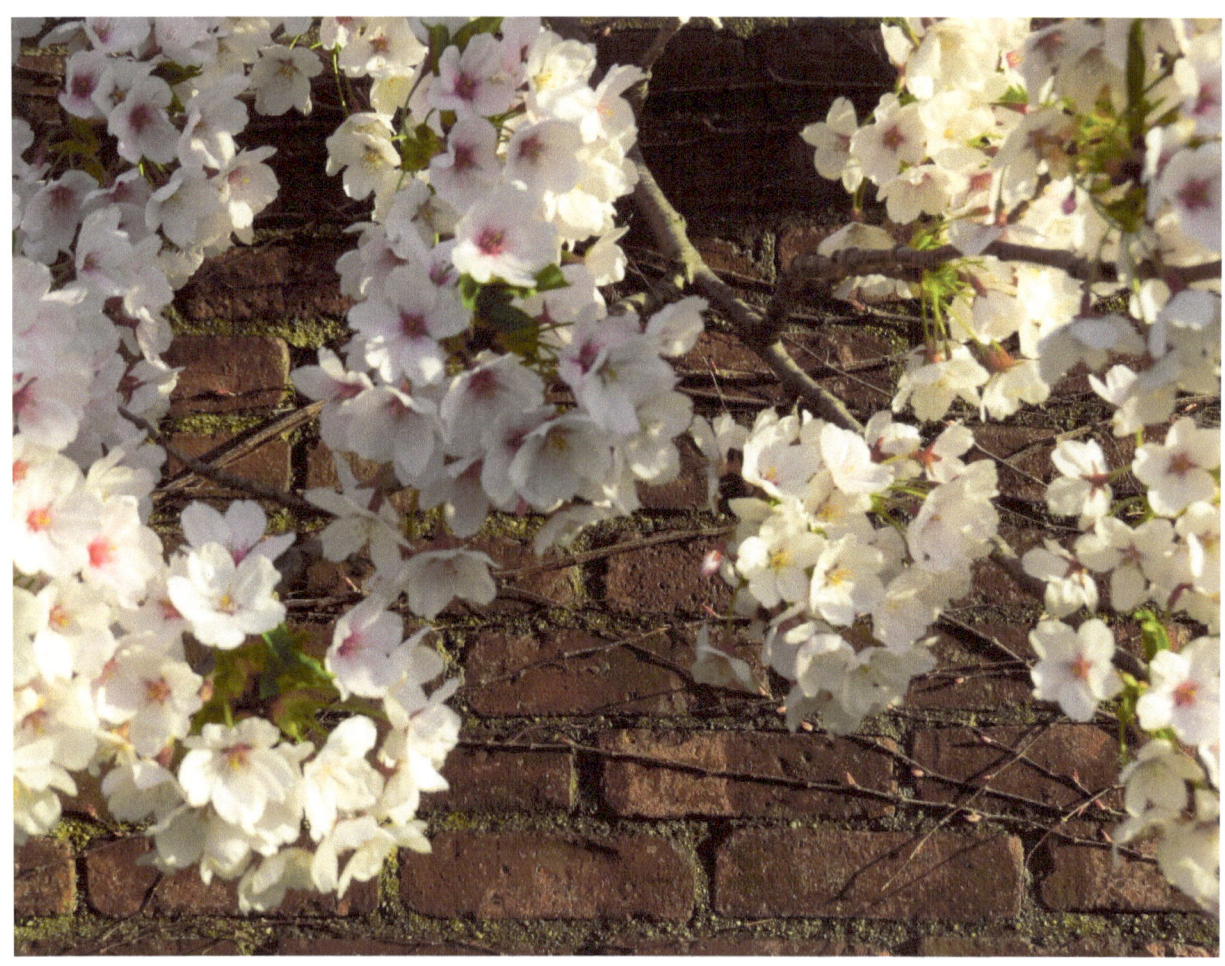

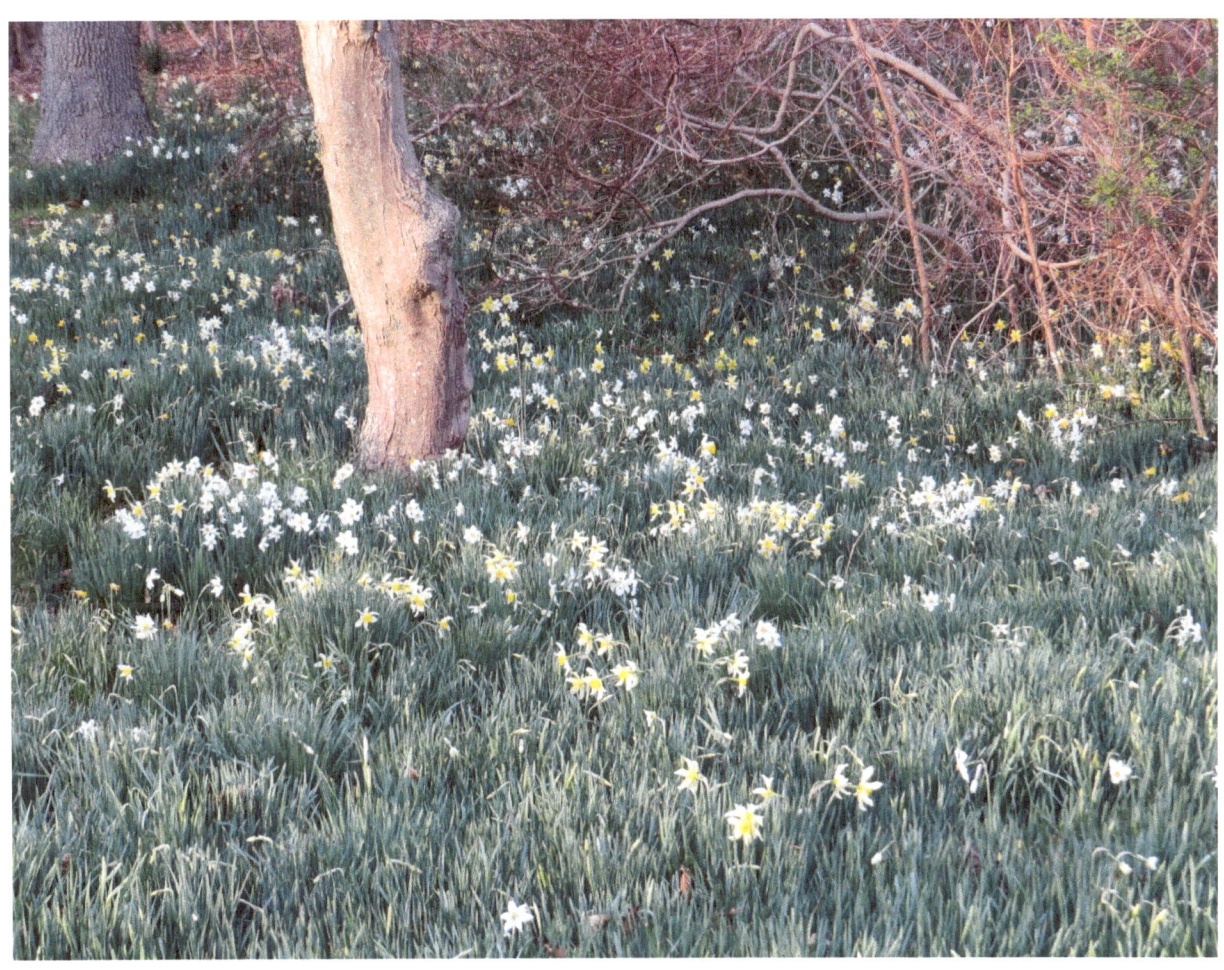

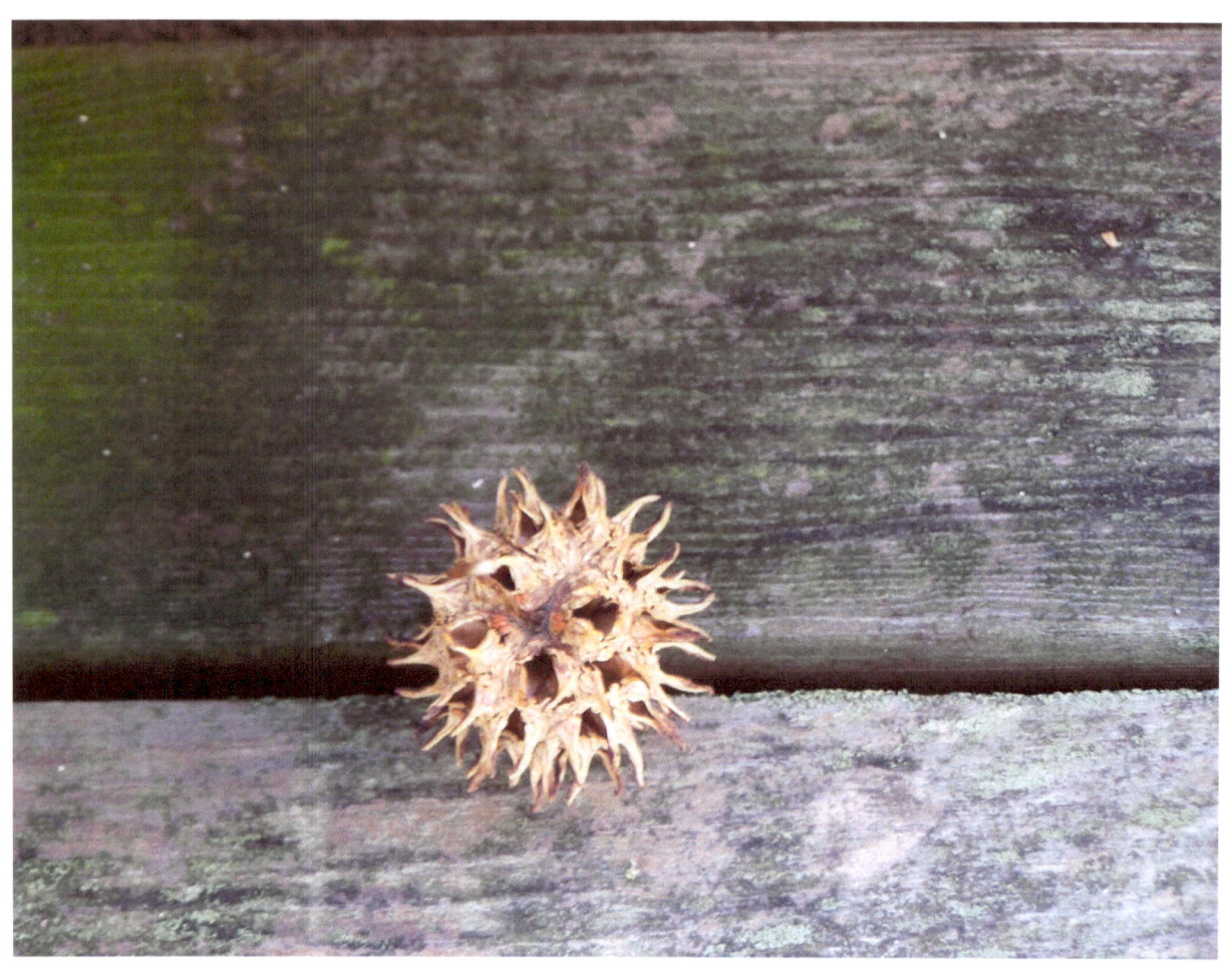

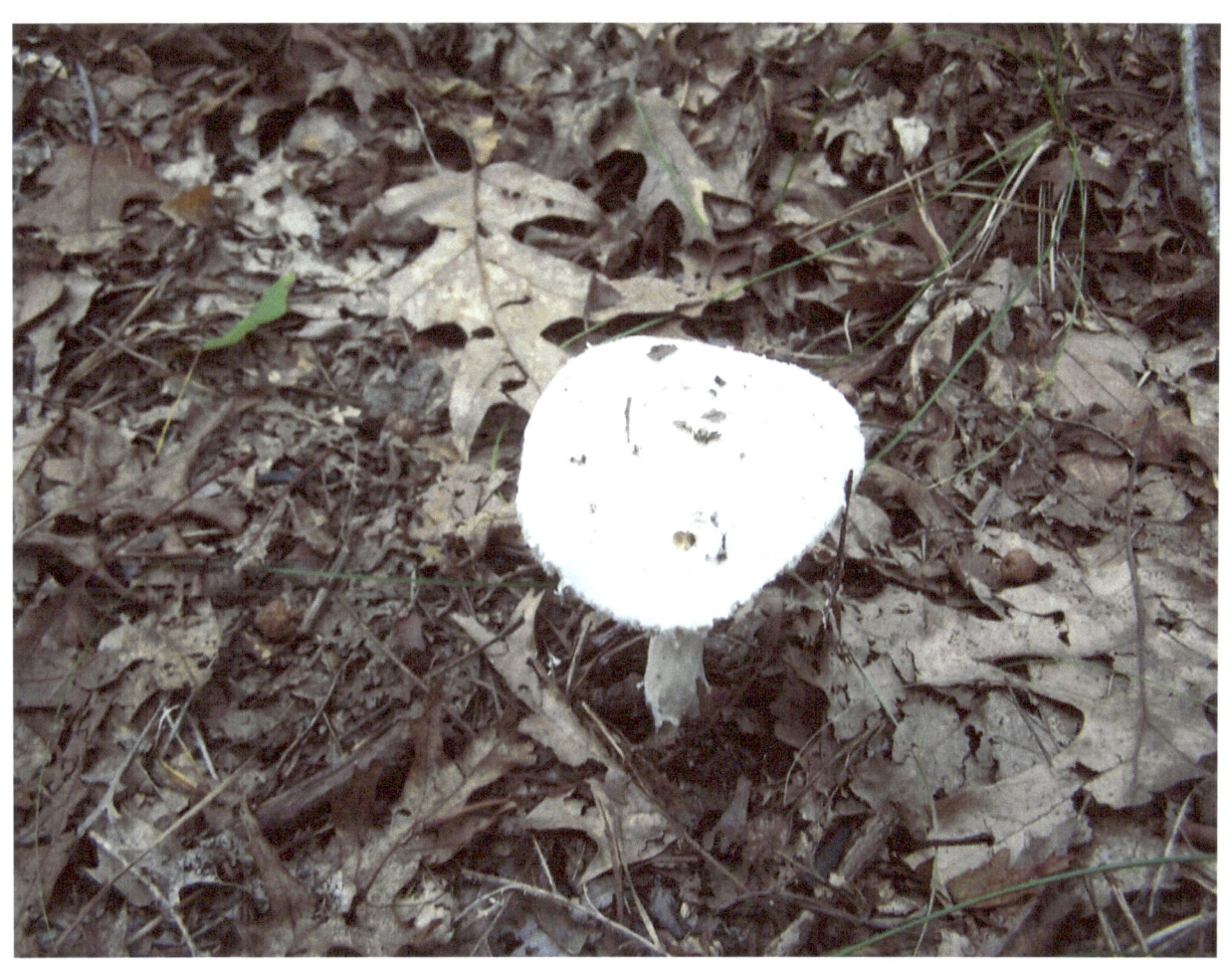

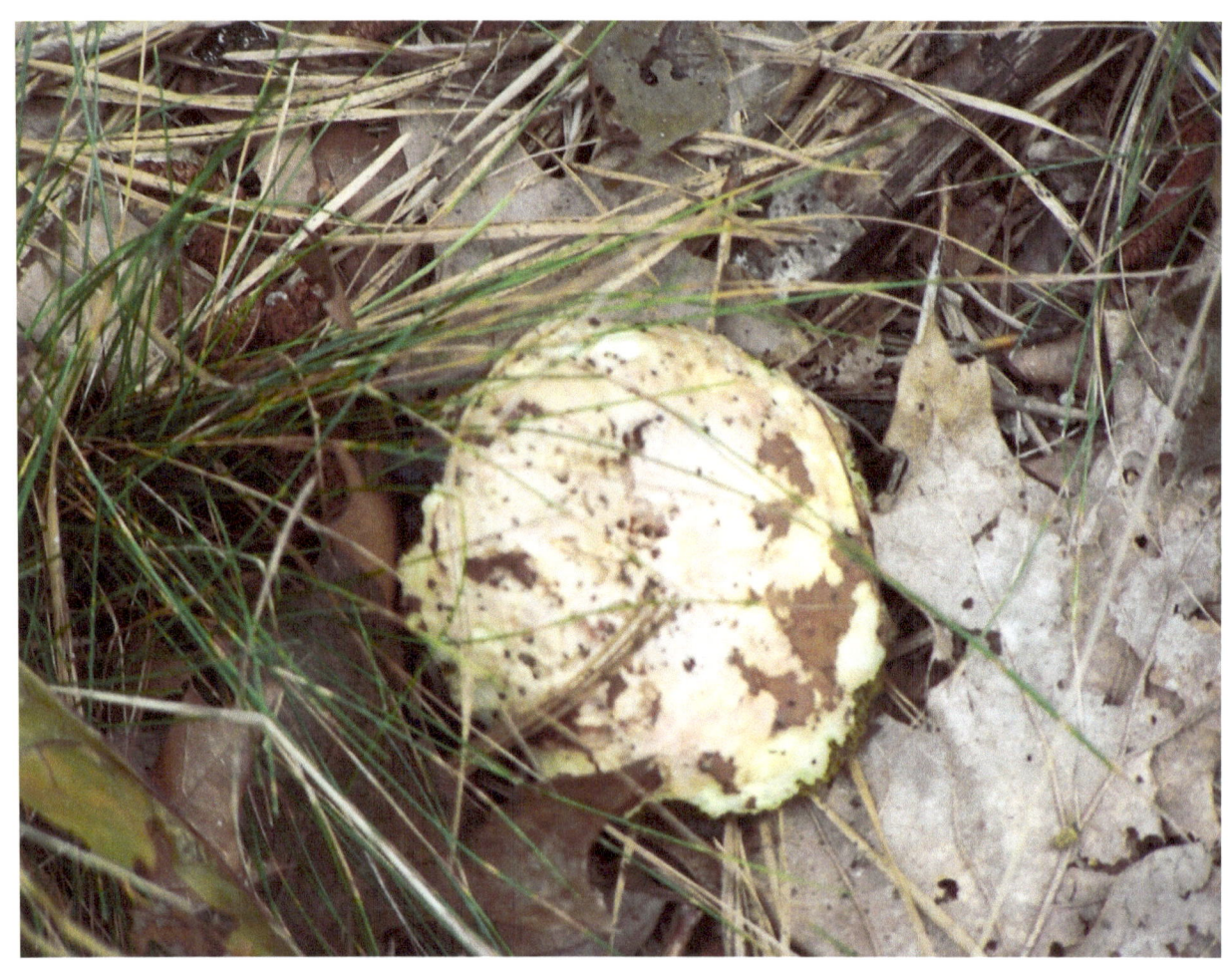

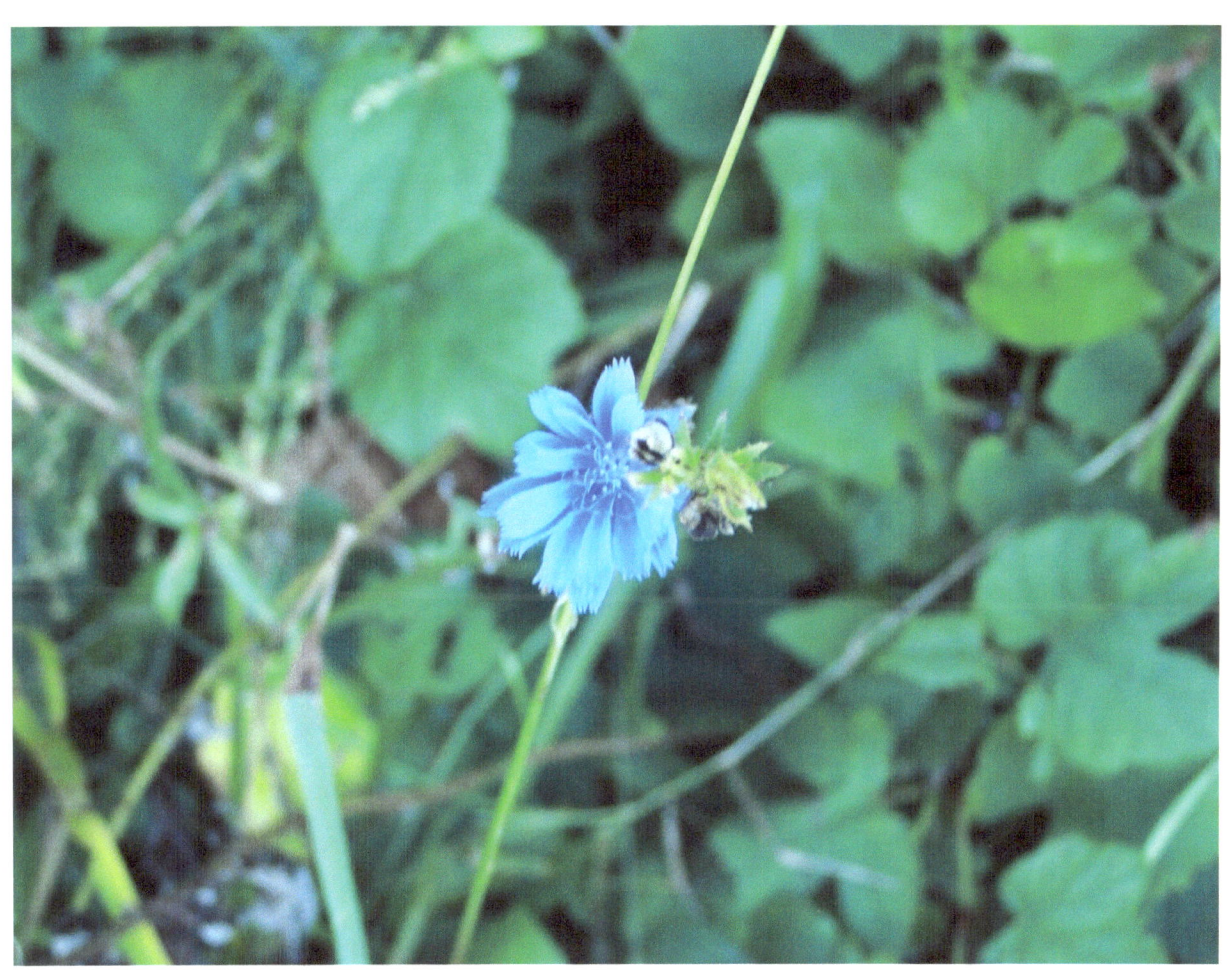

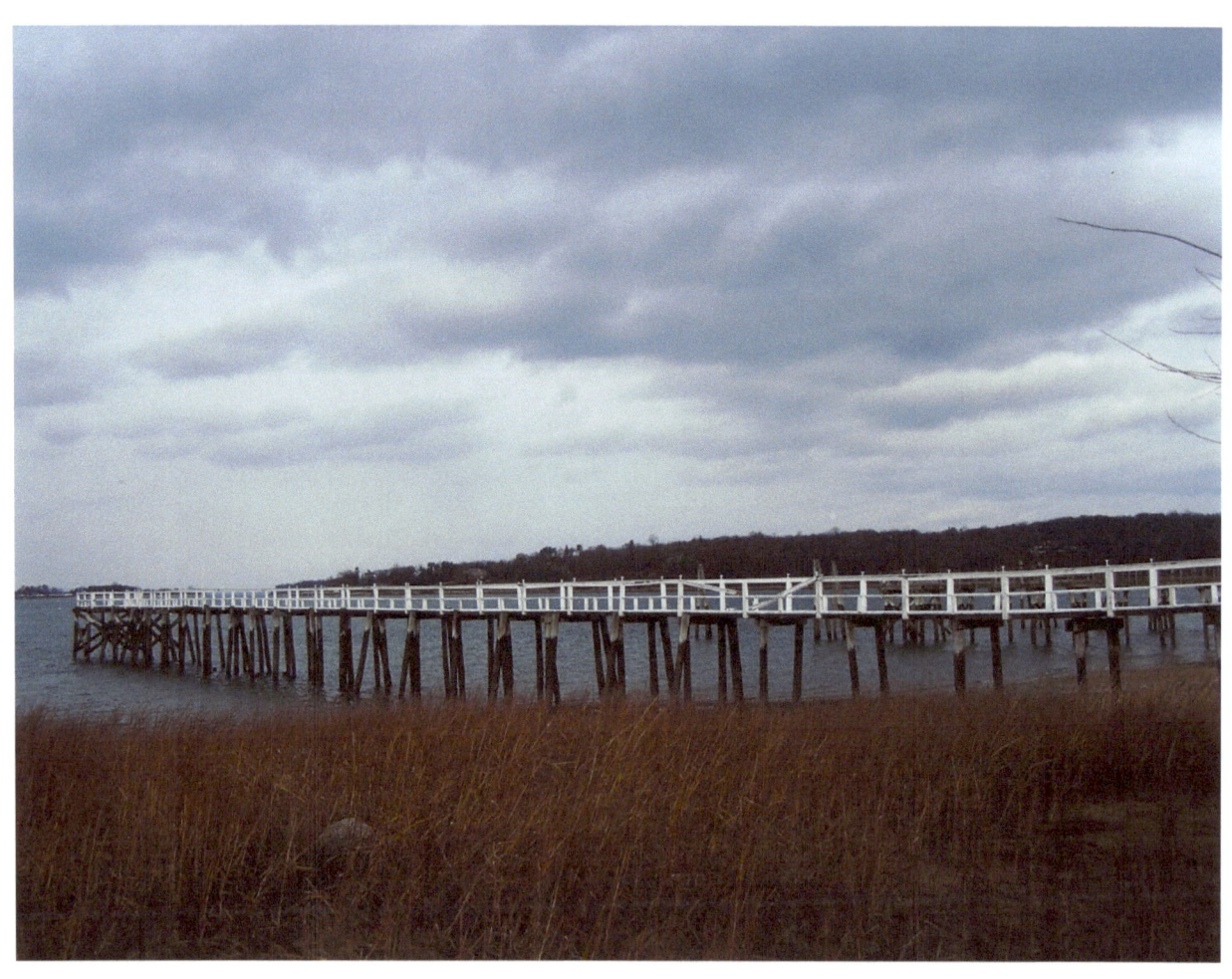

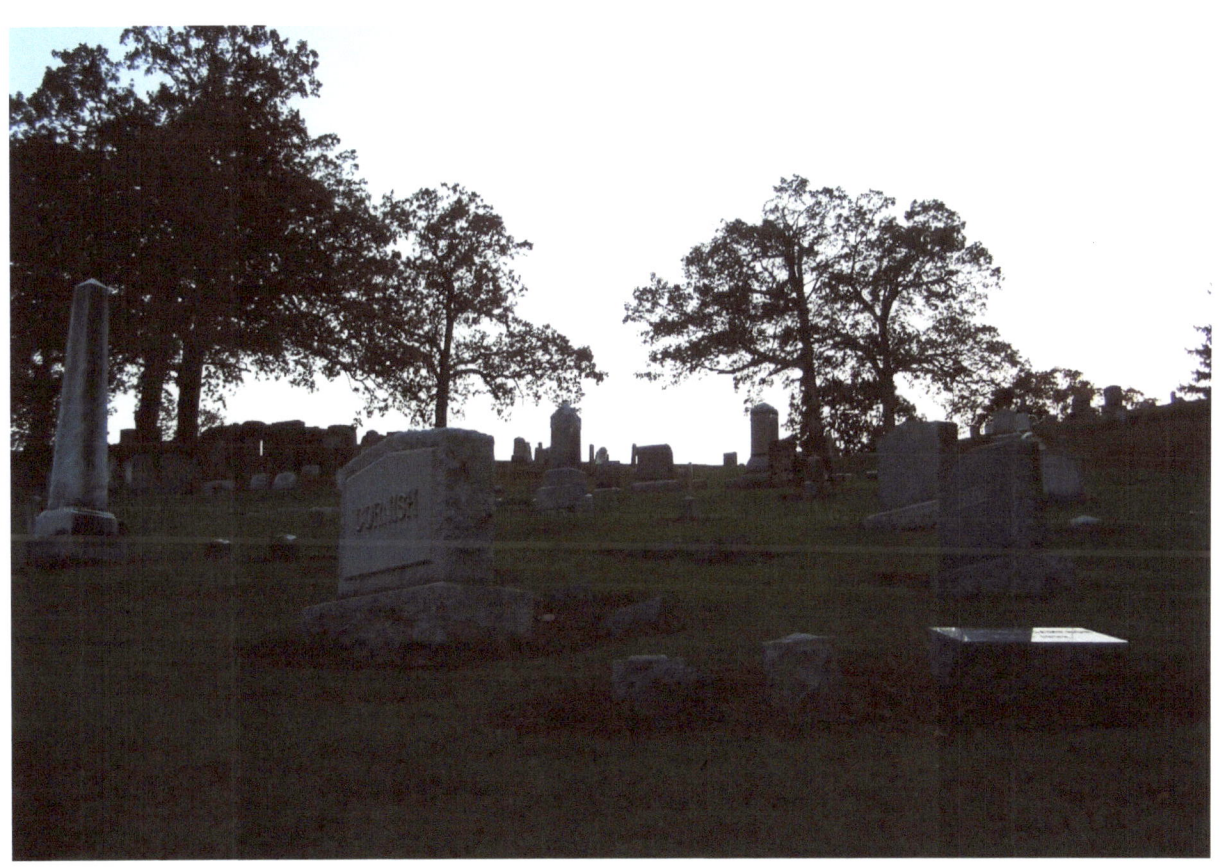

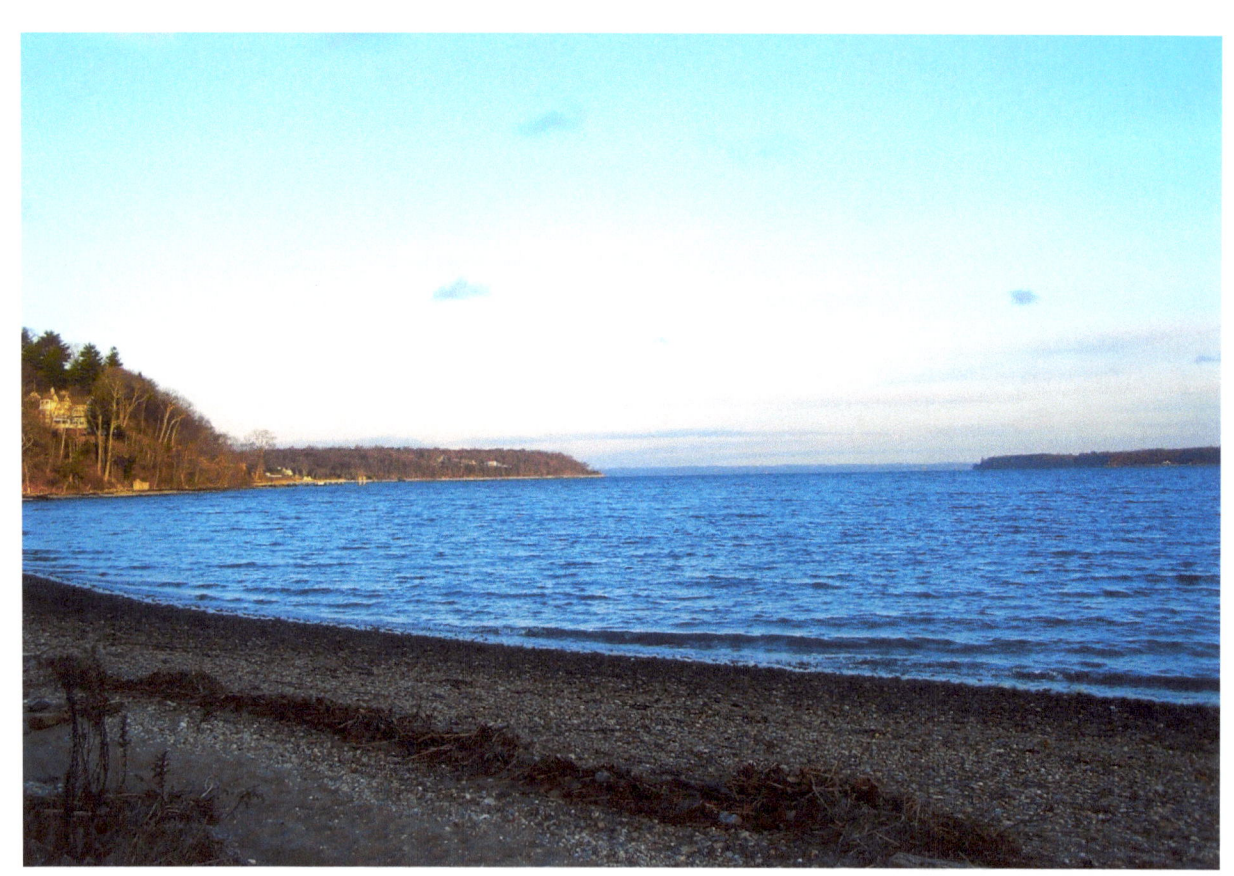

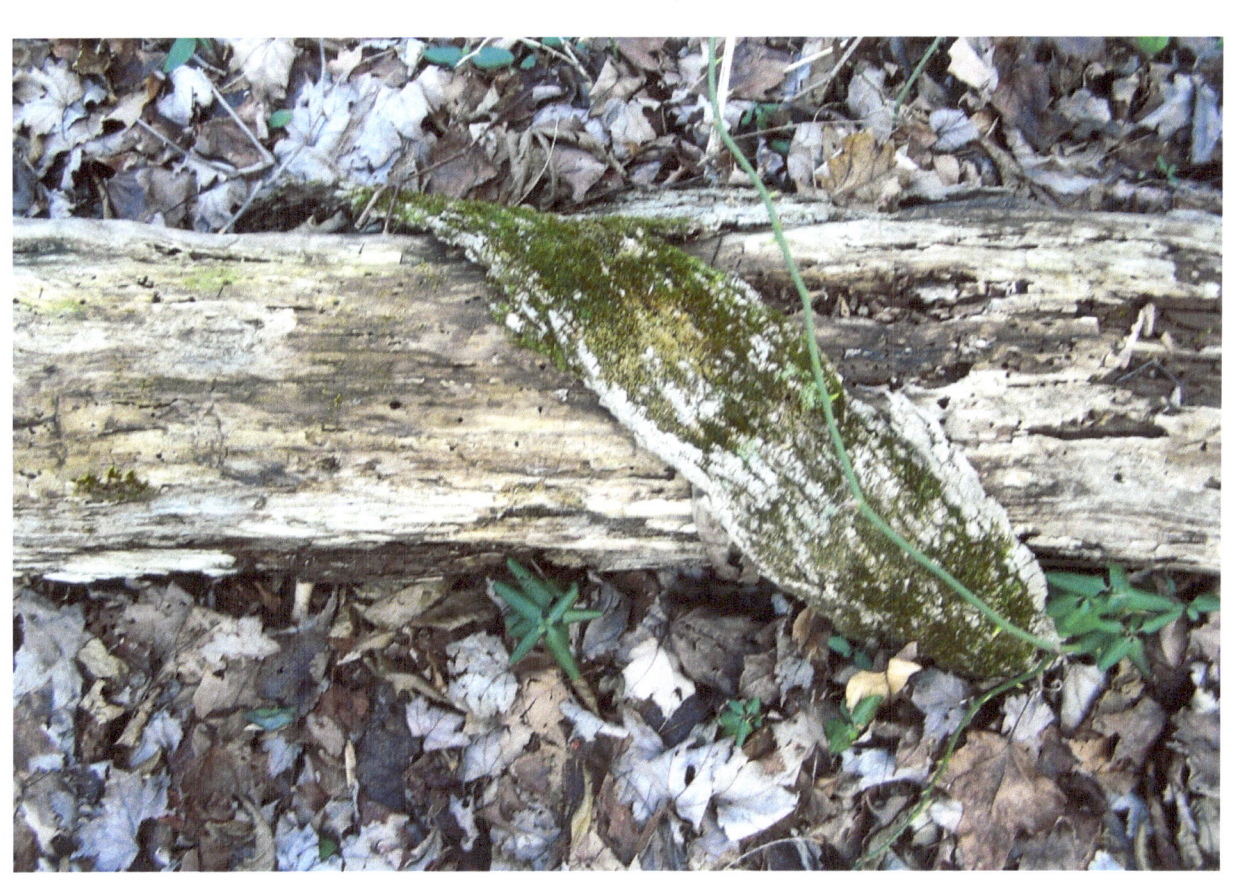

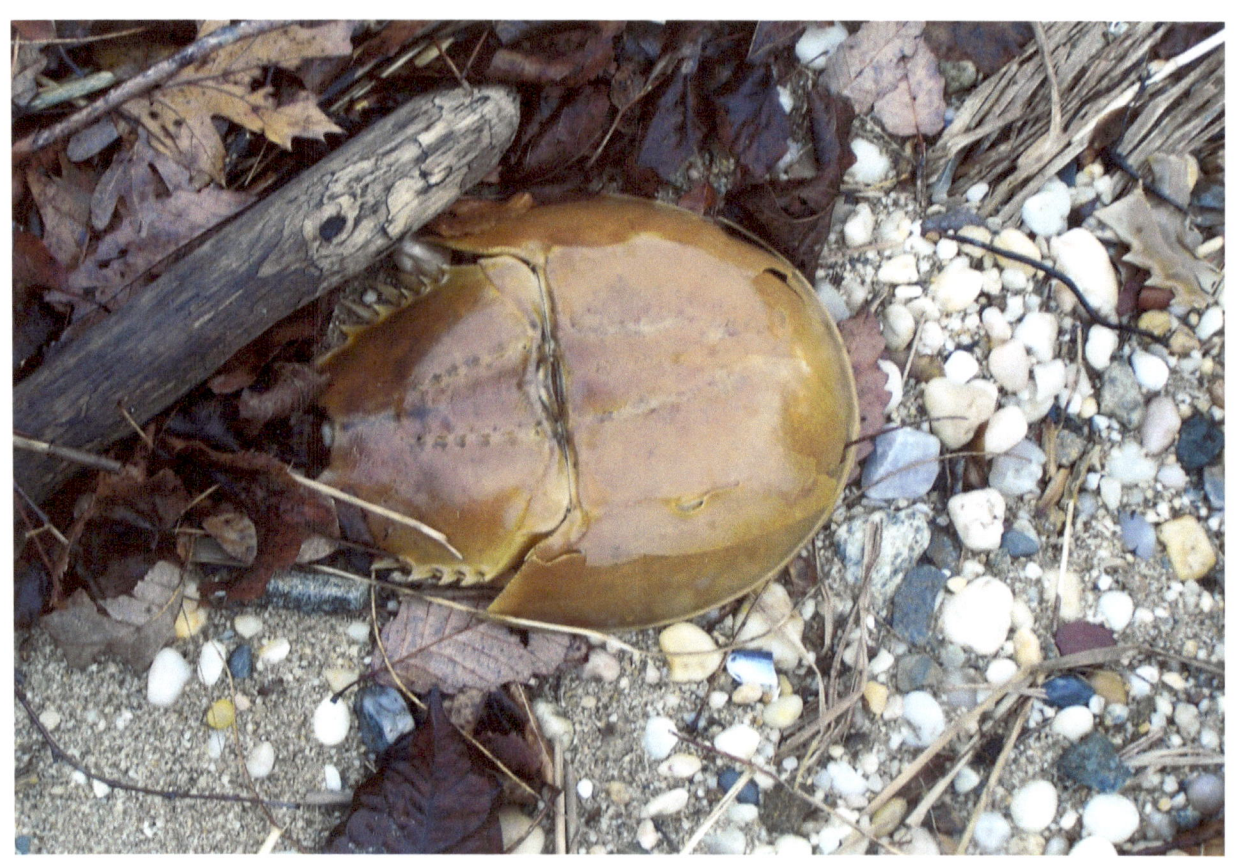

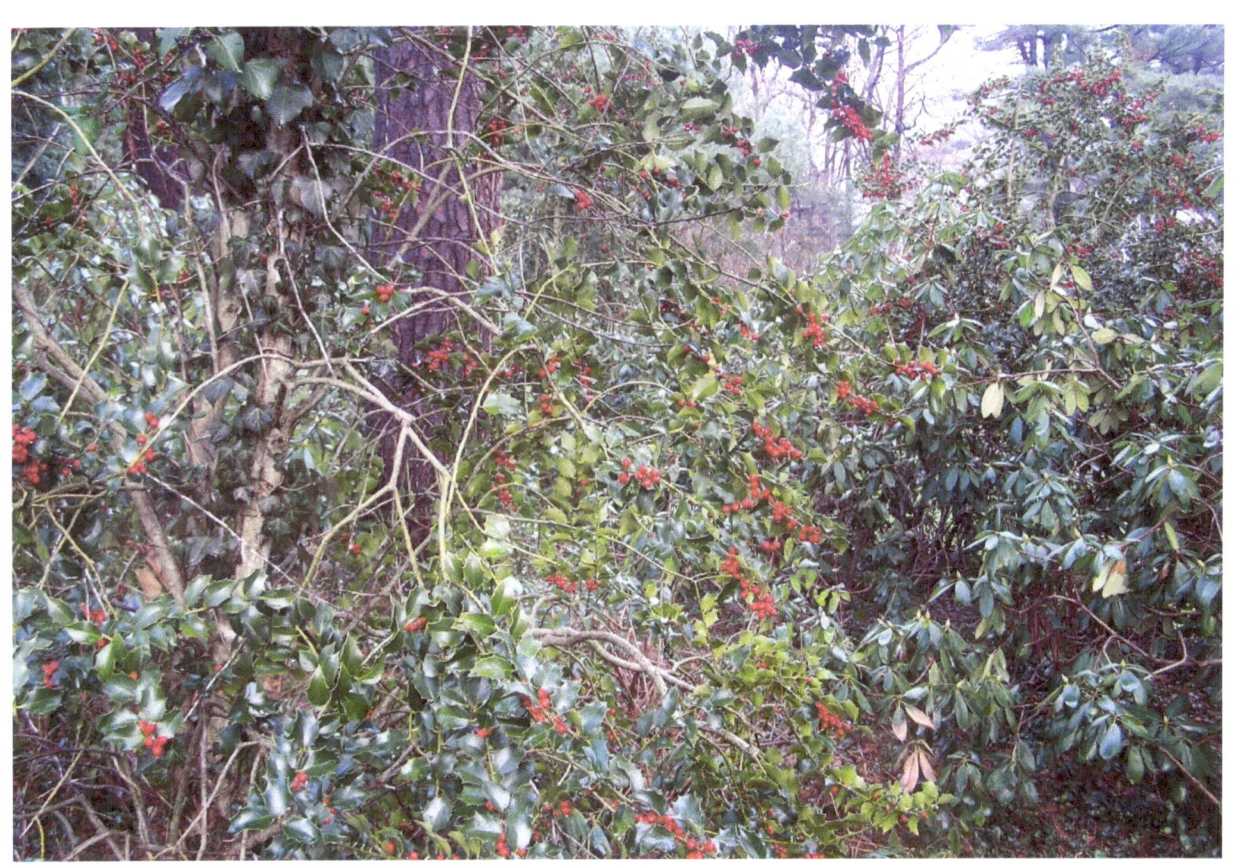

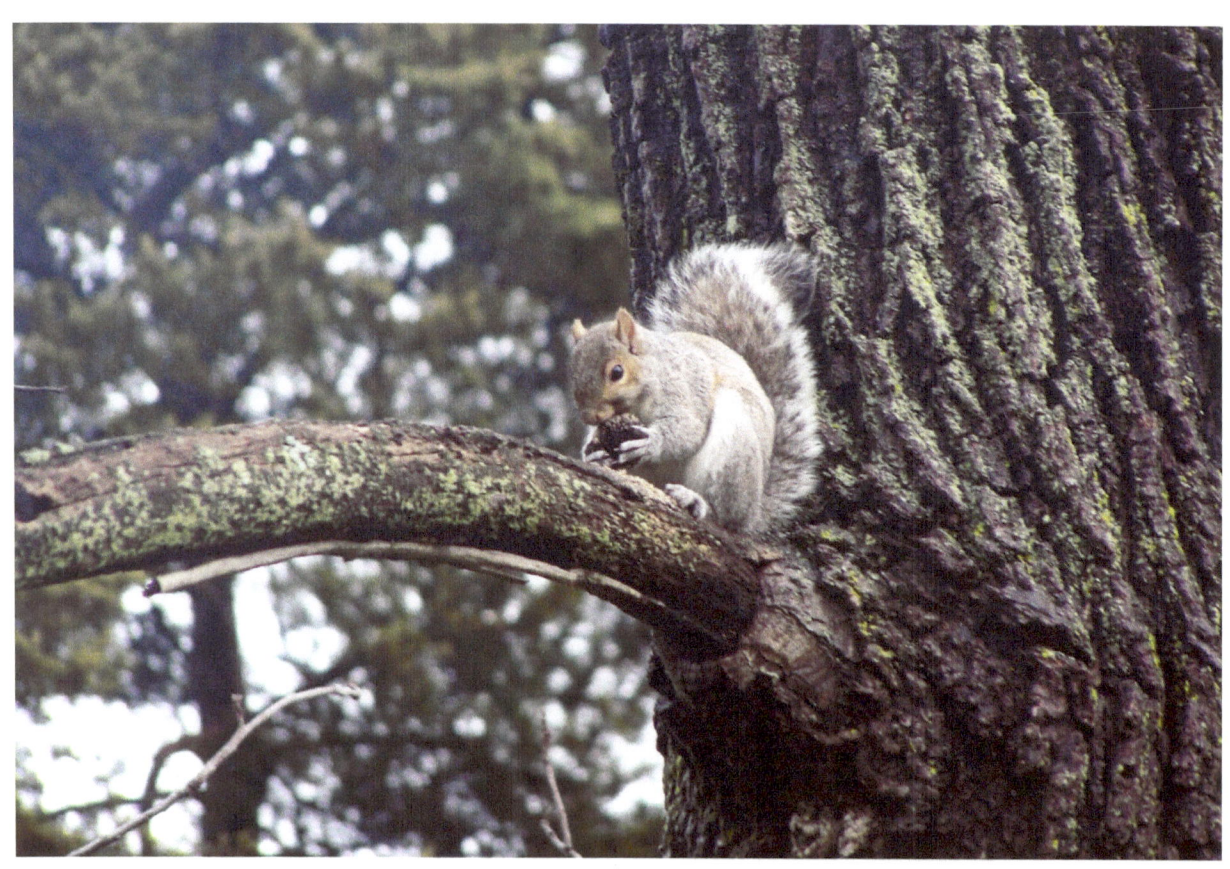

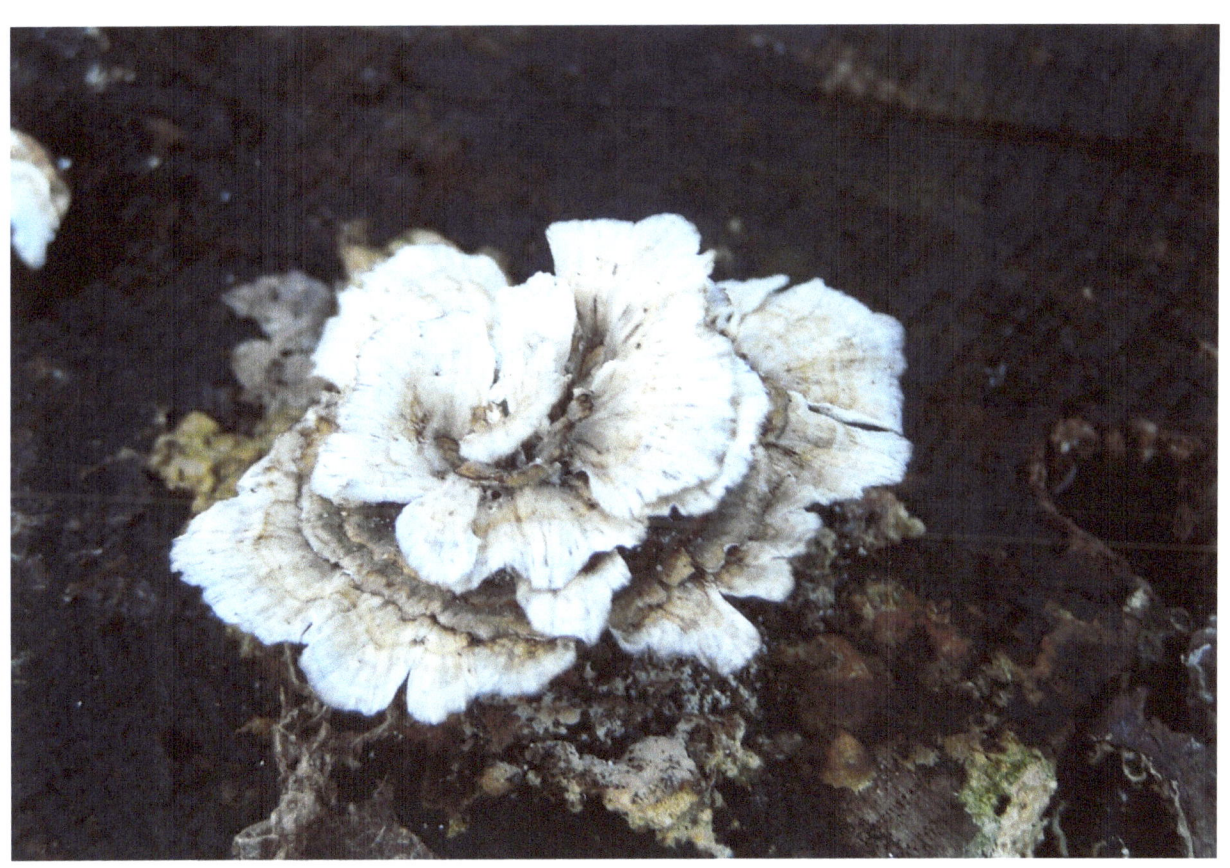

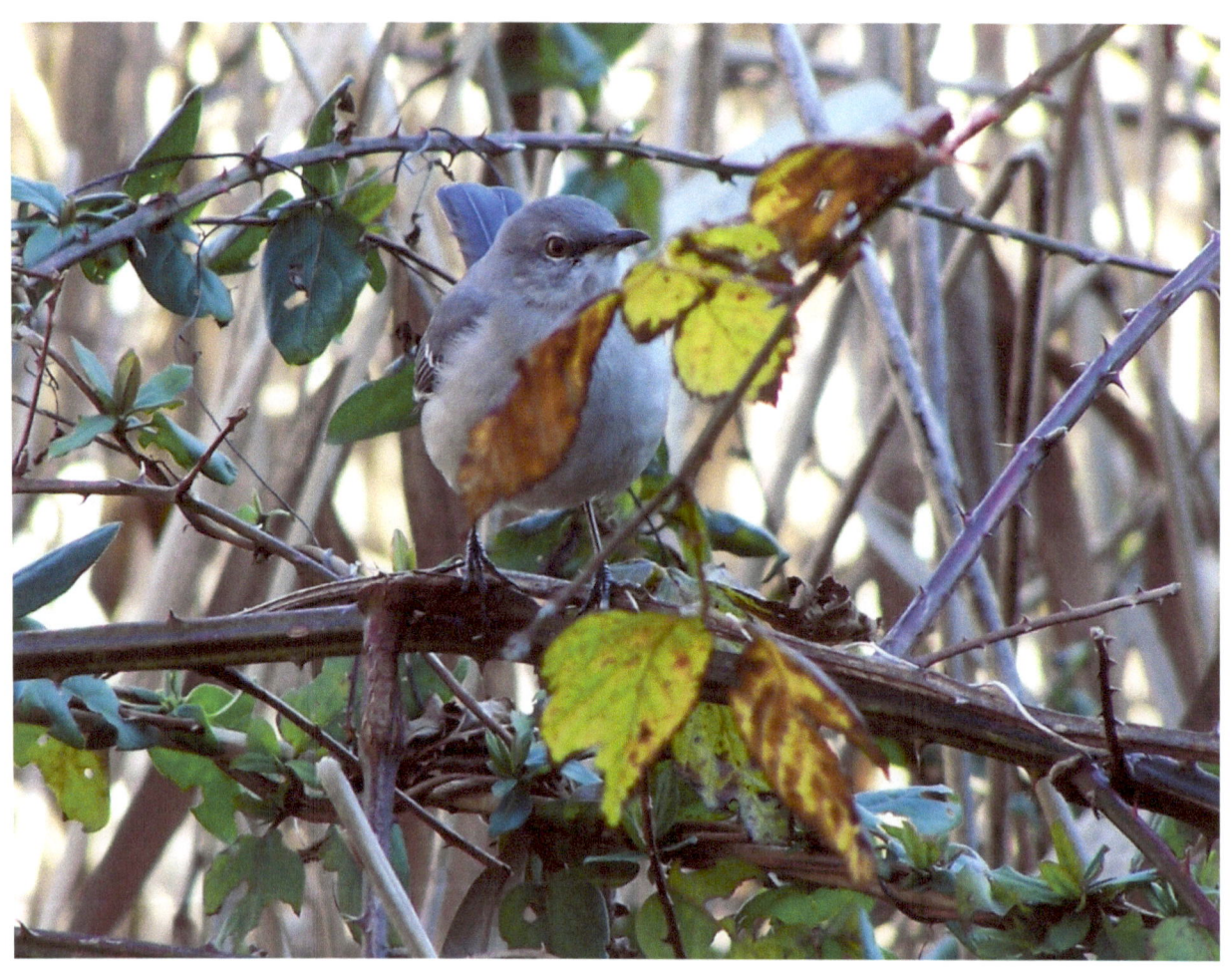

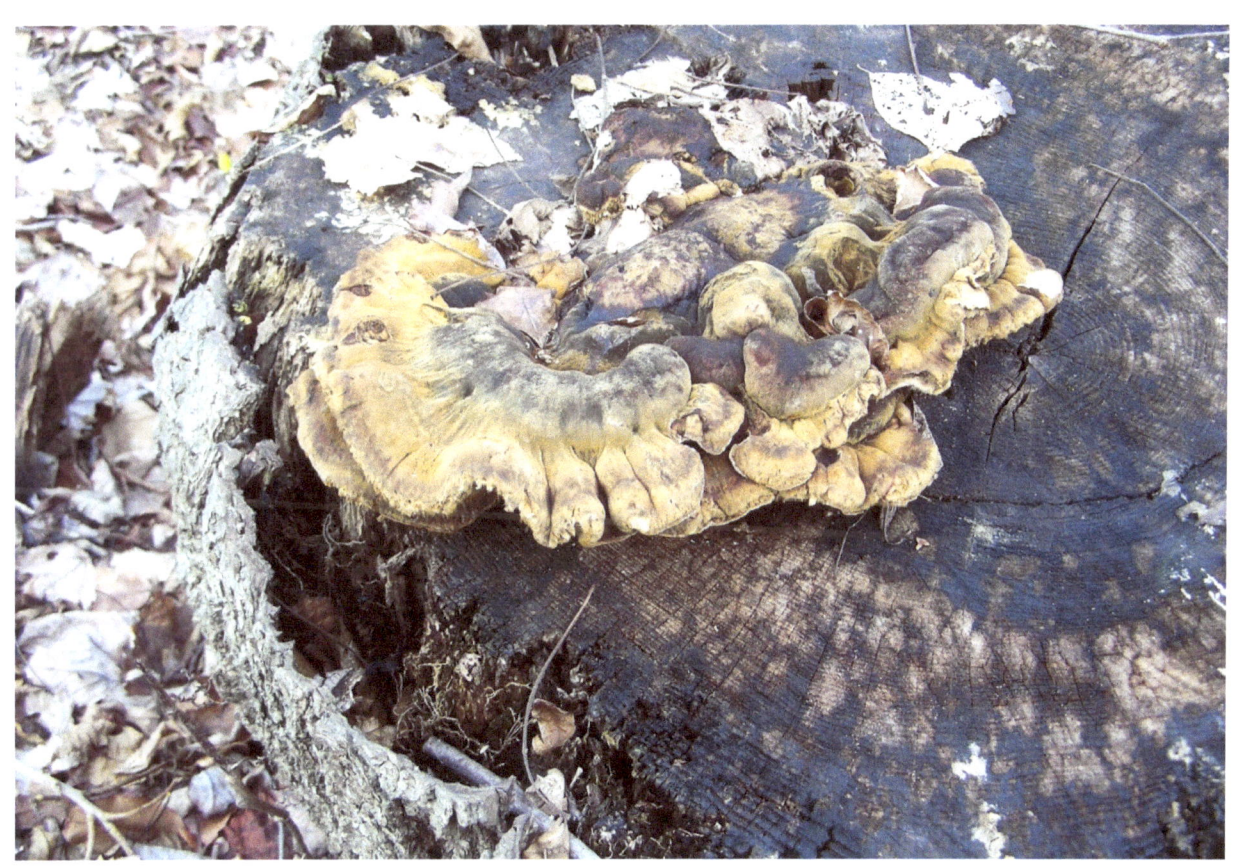

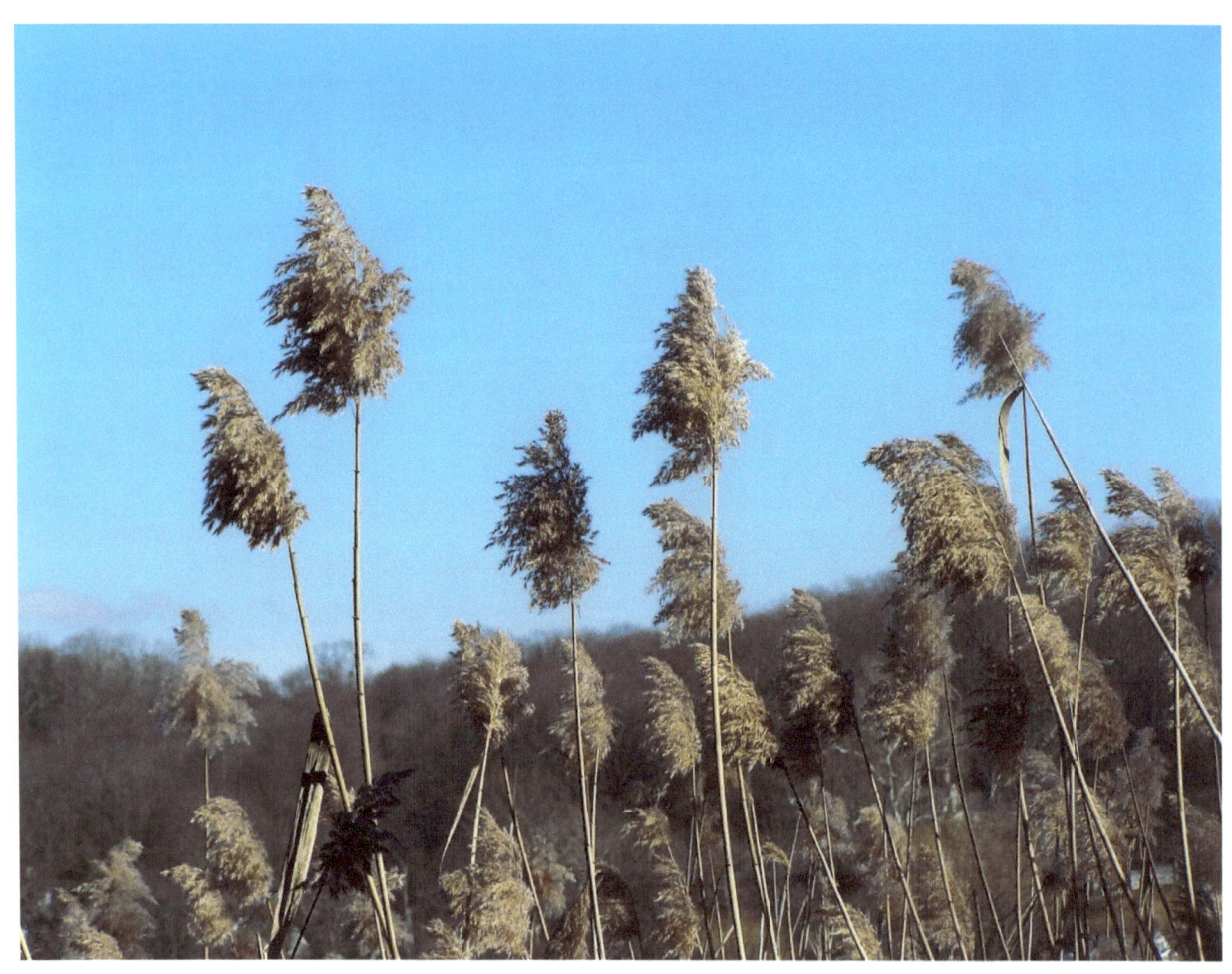

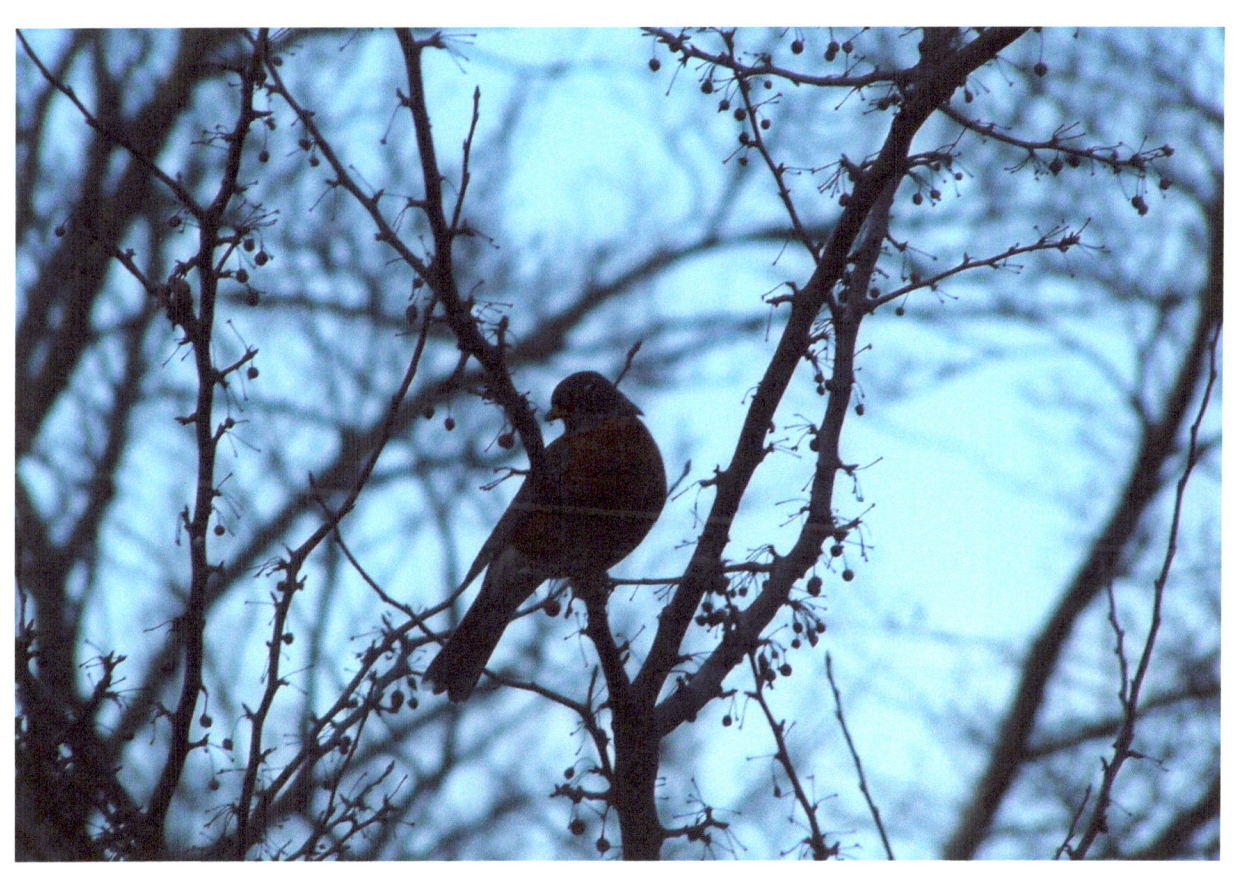

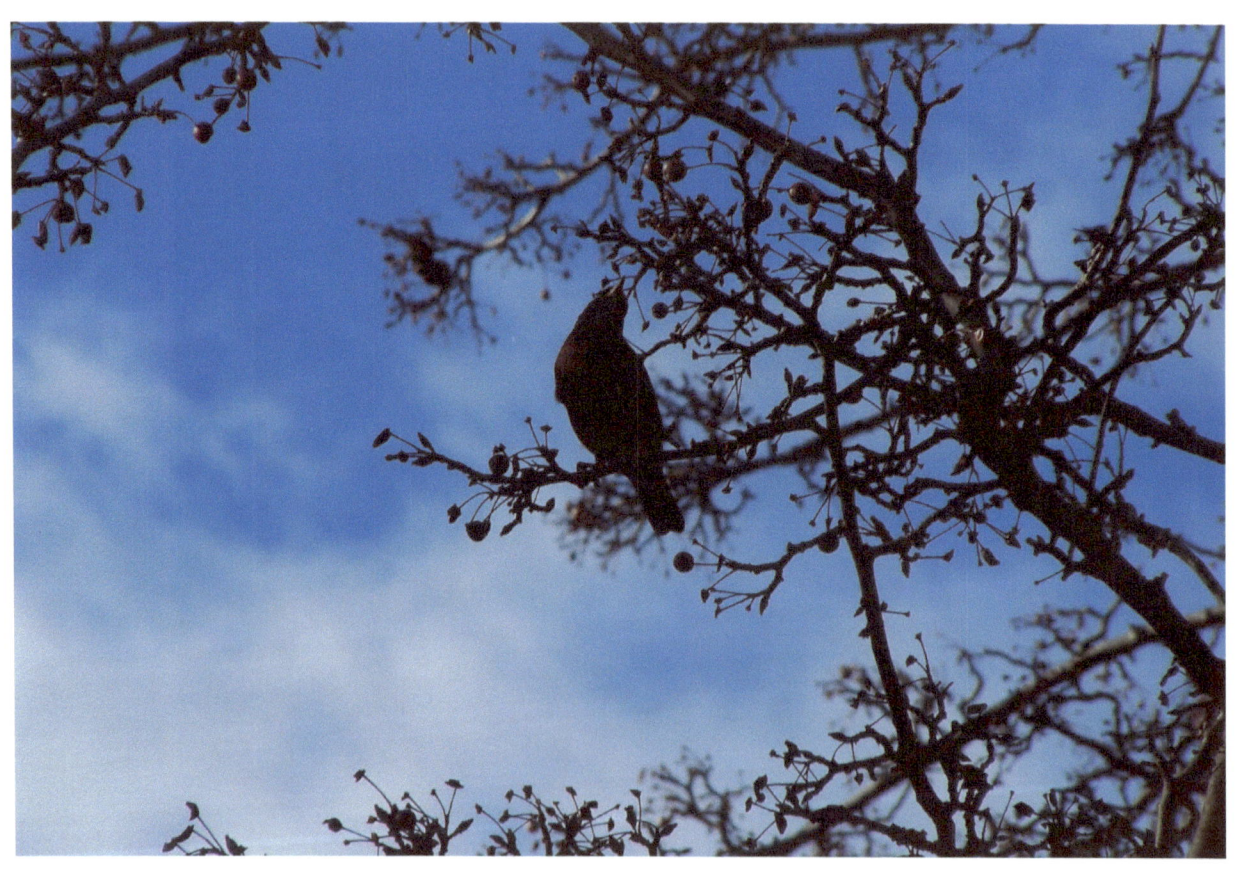

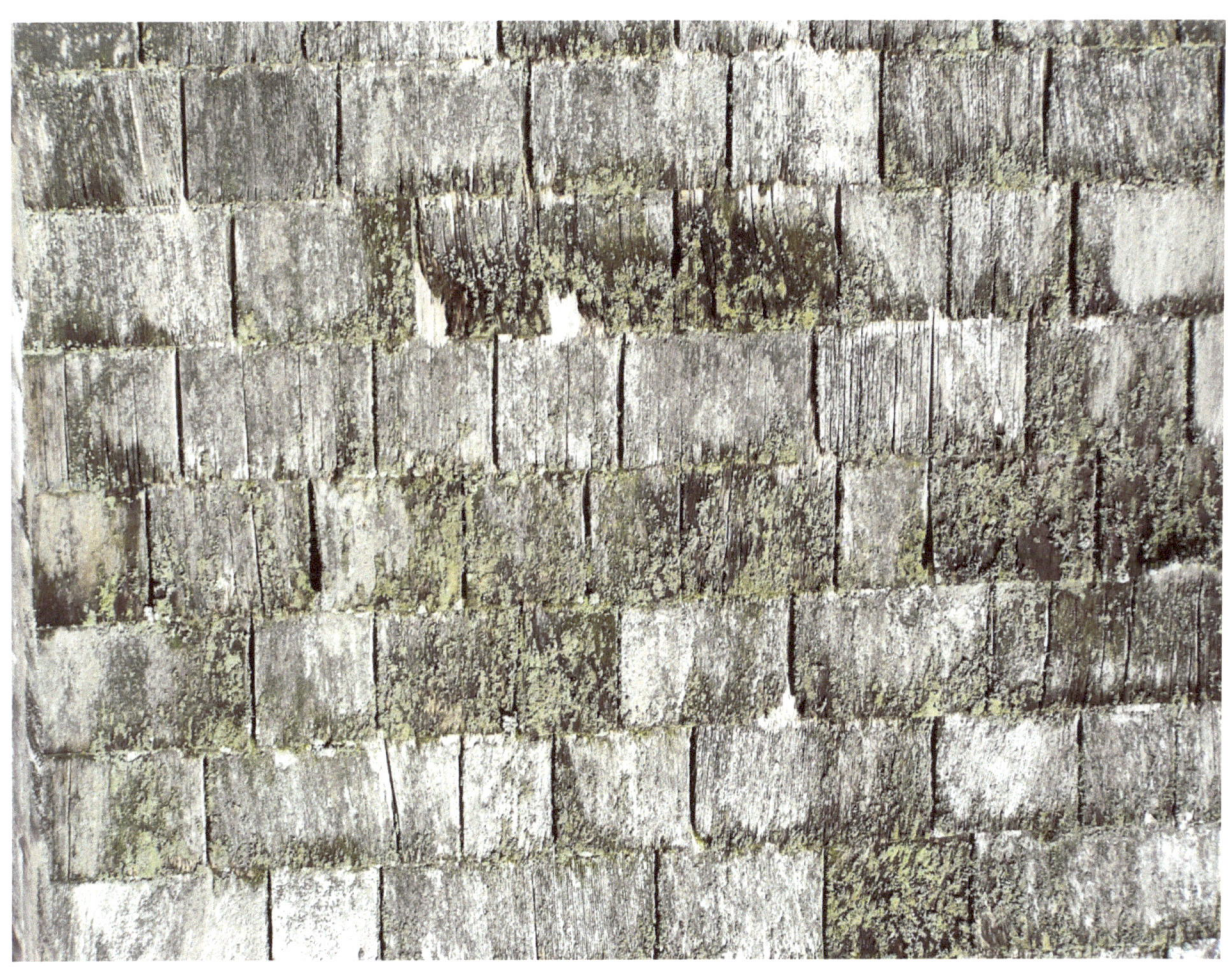

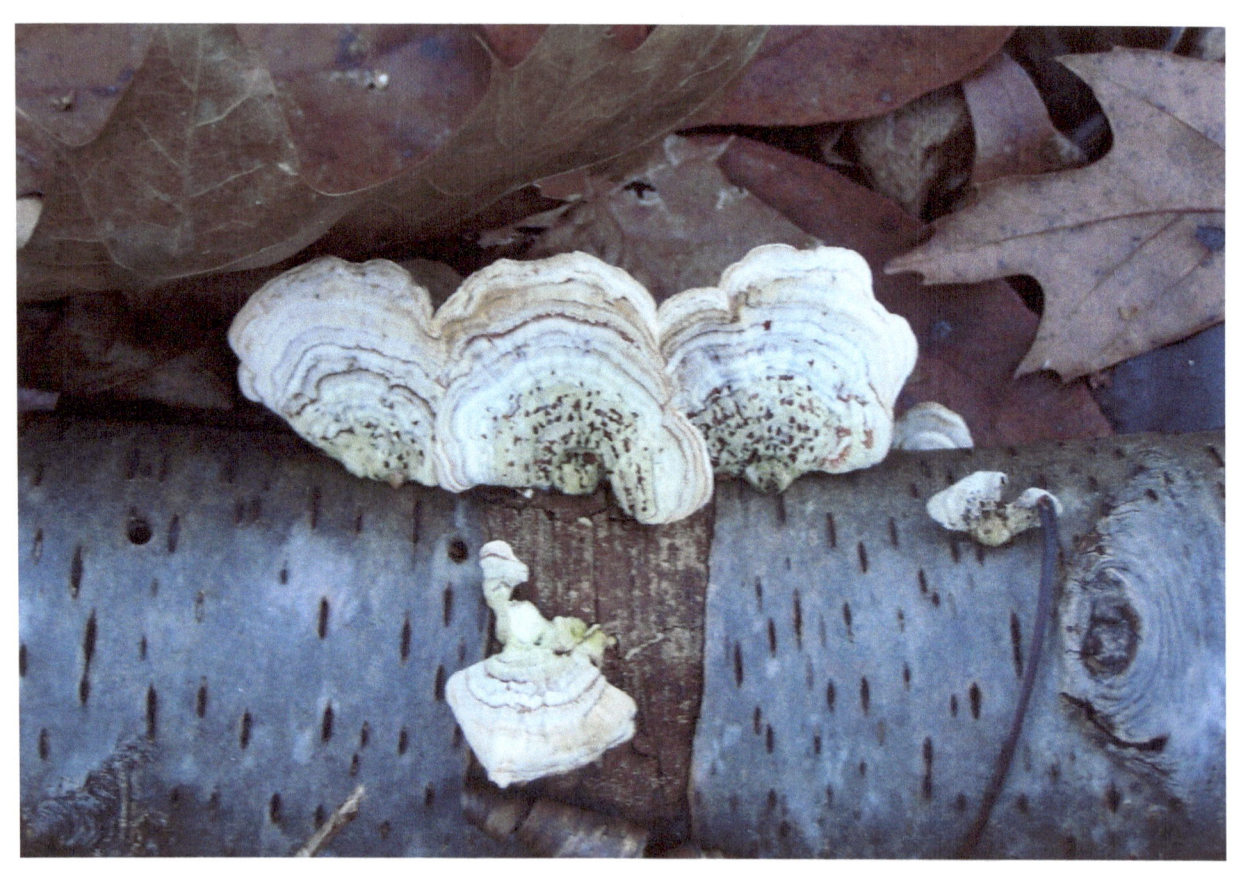

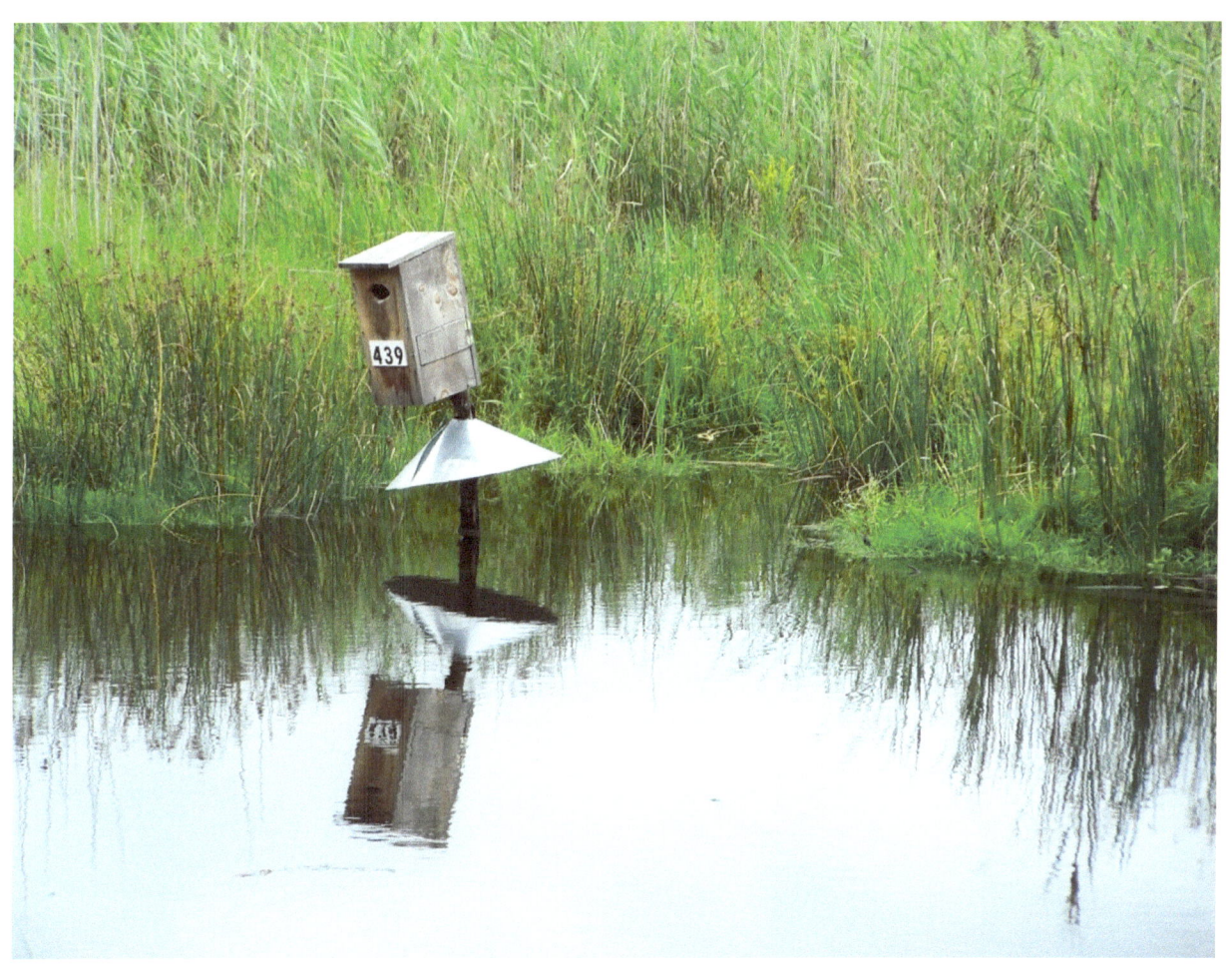

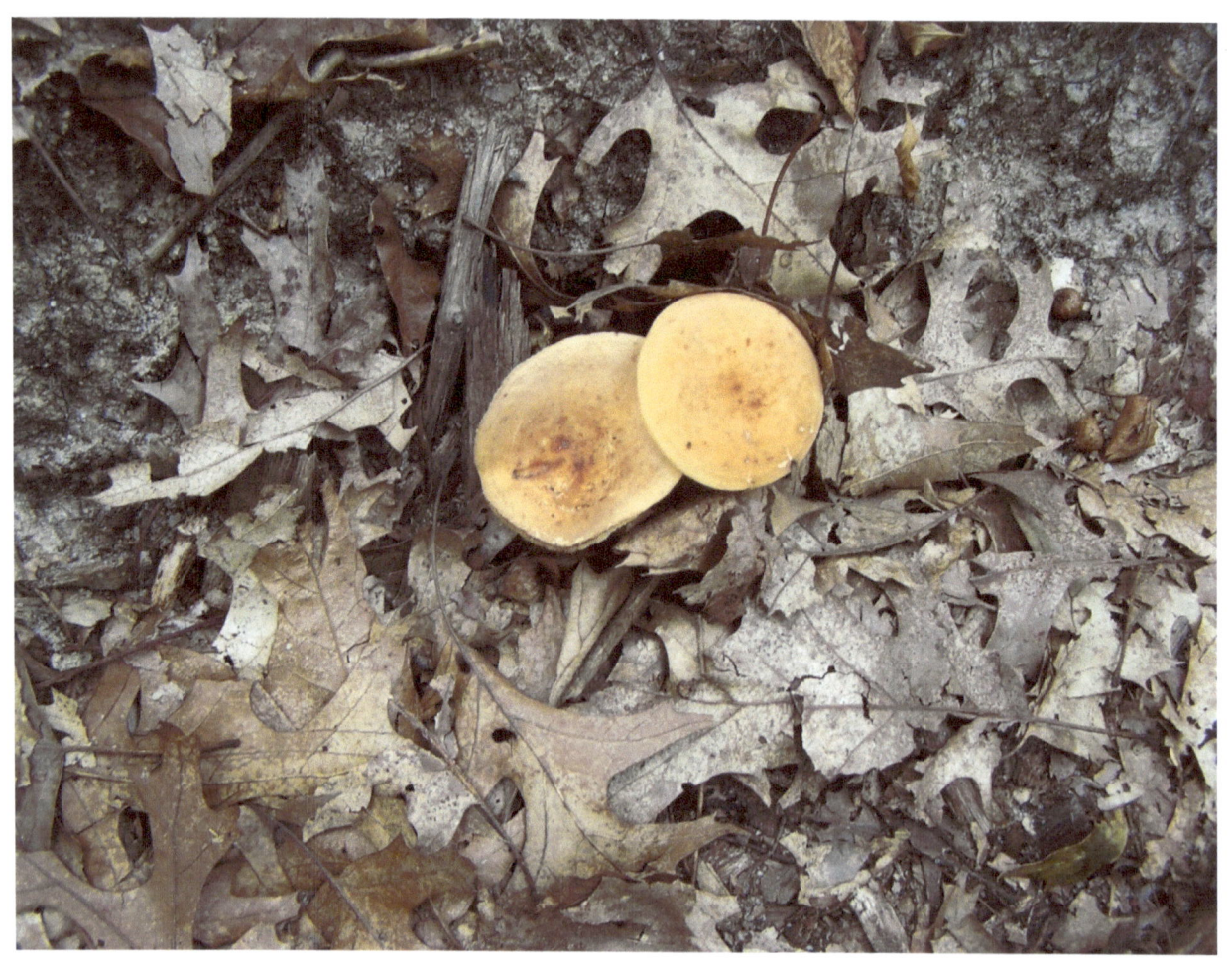

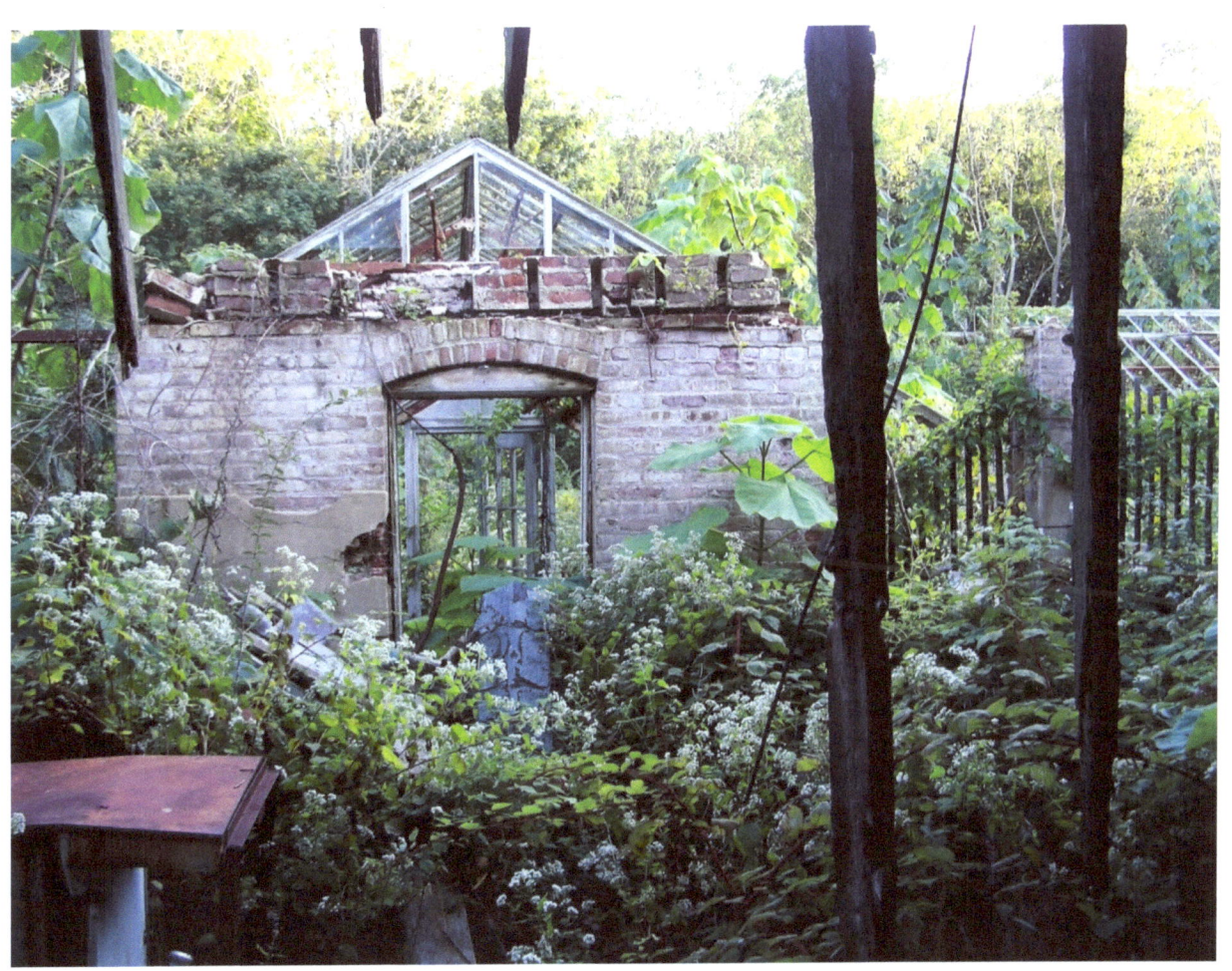

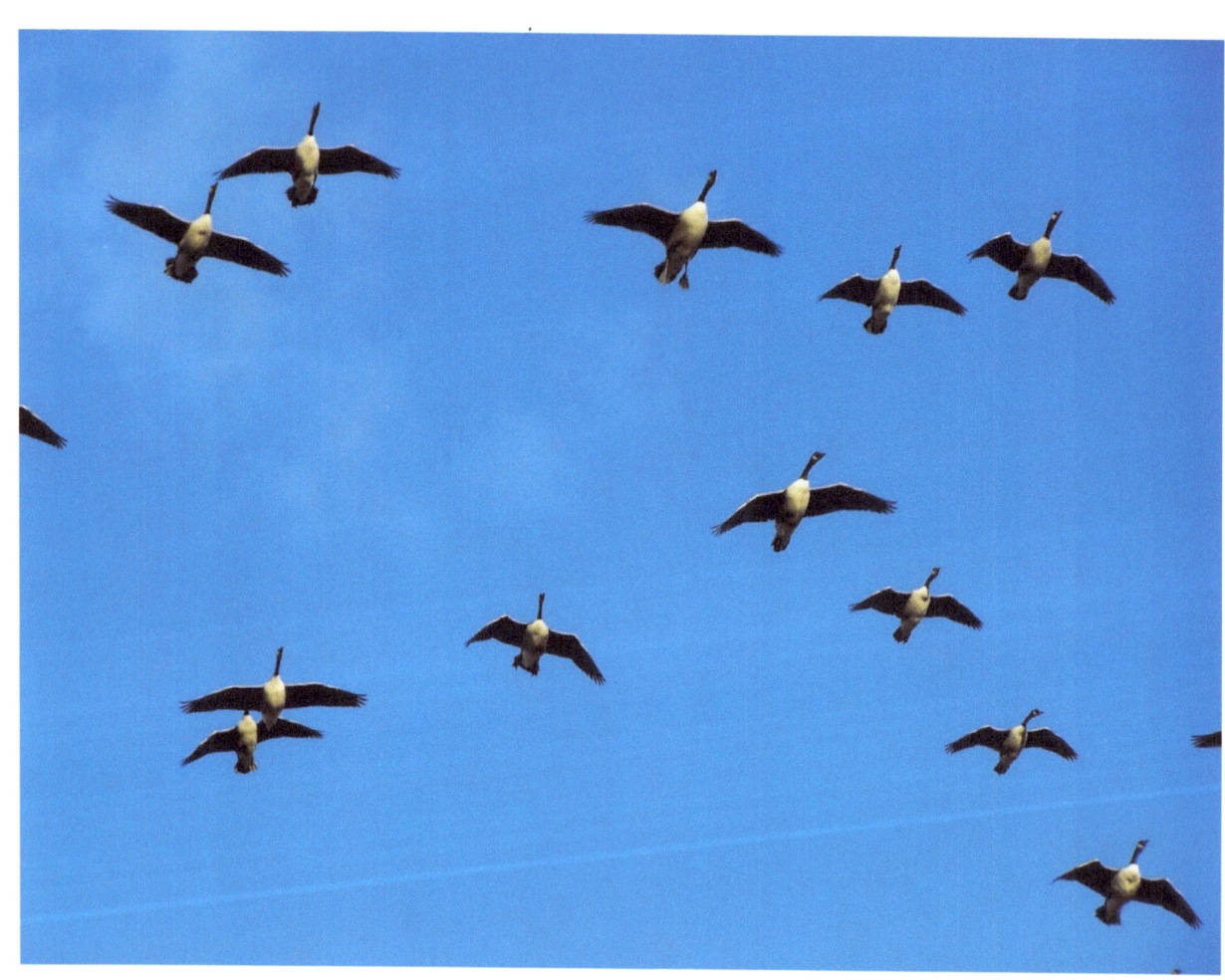

Sukant Khurana is a scientist, artist, writer, and entrepreneur. He was born in Delhi, India and has spent most of his professional career in United States. His science focuses on ameliorating human suffering and coming up with innovative data science solutions, while his art focuses on exploring the human condition. Sukant has worked on efforts to encourage education, sustainable development, women empowerment, environmental, and healthcare issues. In his free time, Sukant can be found working on art projects, traveling off the beaten path, capturing wildlife on his camera or having long chats with friends over a cup of coffee.

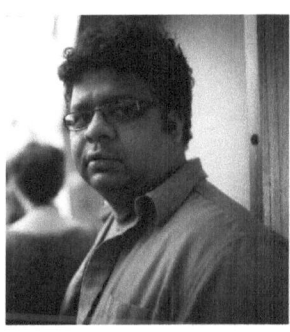